DIANA
COOPER
Transform
Your Life

Other books by Diana Cooper

Light Up Your Life
A Time for Transformation
The Power of Inner Peace
(all Piatkus)

A Little Light on Angels
Golden Footsteps
A Little Light on Ascension

DIANA COOPER

Transform Your Life

A step-by-step programme for change

PIATKUS

To Grahame, teacher of unconditional love, with thanks

© 1993 Diana Cooper

First published in 1993 by
Judy Piatkus (Publishers) Ltd
5 Windmill Street, London W1P 1HF

www.piatkus.co.uk

Reprinted 1996, 1998, 1999

The moral right of the author has been asserted

A catalogue record for this book is
available from the British Library

ISBN 0–7499–1944–2

Designed by Zena Flax
Illustrations by Diana Cooper

Set in $11\frac{1}{2}/14\frac{1}{2}$ Galliard by
Selwood Systems, Midsomer Norton
Printed and bound in Great Britain by
Butler & Tanner Ltd, Frome and London

Contents

Introduction

For much of my life I felt angry, hurt or lonely. Again and again I found myself in difficult situations and relationships without having any idea how I got myself there. Frequently I was ill. I was sure my life ought to have some meaning or purpose but I did not know what to do to change myself or my circumstances. I did not know how to connect with who I was.

At last, after years of seeking and searching, I know how to change my feelings and how to create different situations. I understand who I really am. In this book I share why things happen as they do and how we can change them.

What happens to us in life is a result of our thoughts and beliefs. Our outer experiences are a faithful reflection of what is going on internally. Even when we know this, many of us still do not know how to change ourselves. I often hear: 'I know my inner child is hurting but what can I do?' or 'I know I've attracted this situation but how can I change it?' or 'I want to love but I don't know how to'. The following exercises show you how.

The exercises, meditations, visualisations and drawings are designed to expand our perspectives so that we can change the beliefs and attitudes which create our problems. As our attitudes to people and situations change, they respond differently to us and our lives become harmonious.

There are two ways to use the book. Either start at the beginning and work through the exercises, which will expand your consciousness step by step, or look up your problem, read how it is created and do the appropriate exercise whenever you need to. For instance if you feel overburdened and unappreciated, look up 'The martyr'. Read how you have placed yourself in this position. Do the exercises and take the decision to change. If you have a frozen shoulder, look up 'Shoulders' in the 'Transform Your Body' section and work from there.

I suggest you keep an exercise book to record insights or pictures that come up for you. Date the exercises as you do them. When you repeat something six months later, you will be surprised at the change in yourself.

You are part of the divine energy and the intention of this book is to re-align you with your truth. You are a unique and powerful Spiritual Being who has come into a body for this human experience. It is time to transform your life by re-awakening the memory of who you really are.

Diana Cooper
July 1993

Your beliefs

I believe that we can all transform our lives if we really want to do so. Most of us sense that we have creativity, power and potential within us that we don't know how to find.

This workbook is filled with exercises to facilitate the process of change. When we understand how to make these changes and take full responsibility for what we are creating, then we achieve mastery over our lives.

Most people who are attracted to this book will know that we create our own reality with our thoughts and beliefs. When we change our beliefs, our lives automatically change too.

It works like this. The unconscious mind is a computer. Each of us brings into this life our own individual beliefs based on the evolution of our soul and our past life experiences. *So we are born with our basic program. This is our belief system or mind set.*

We then interpret everything, *including* how our parents treat us and what they say to us, according to our computer program.

One person holds the belief that she is pretty. If someone tells her how attractive she is, she smiles, accepts the compliment and feels even better about herself.

Another person believes she is unattractive. When she receives a compliment, she either doesn't hear it and it doesn't even register as a compliment or she rejects it. She'll probably say something like 'Oh don't be silly.' She may even think the other person is laughing at her and take it as an insult! Either way she won't record the compliment in the computer of her unconscious mind.

Our self-esteem and confidence are based on our beliefs.

Our happiness depends on our self-esteem and confidence.

Our health depends on our happiness.

When we send misery messages to our bodies, the cells of our bodies close down in fear and create physical problems. When we send happy messages to our bodies, the cells of our bodies create health.

We are all whole and healthy in the mind of God. So perfect health and wholeness are our divine right.

In the process of change, the first step is to bring things to conscious awareness. We can't change anything we aren't aware of. Throughout this book we will be using spontaneous drawings, visualisations and awareness exercises to bring things to consciousness.

And we will be learning a variety of techniques, including affirmations, creative visualisation, dynamic drawing and writing, to anchor the new positive, empowering beliefs which change our lives.

1 What negative messages did you *hear* from your mother, father, grandparents or teachers about your ability, your attractiveness, your body, how lovable you were, the outside world? *Write a list* of the basic unhelpful beliefs which create your life:

_____

_____

2 Now *write down* the opposite. These are the positive beliefs which you must focus on and constantly re-affirm.

_____

_____

3 With these new beliefs, how different will your life be? *Write down* a few of the changes which will automatically occur:

_____

_____

Confidence

Every single one of us believes that we are not good enough. The bigger our not-good-enough belief is, the more difficult our life becomes, as we have no sense of confidence or self-worth.

If our not-good-enough feelings are outweighed by positive feelings of self-esteem, then we will succeed and be relaxed and calm about life.

Only a person who lacks confidence in themself is patronising or sarcastic. So if someone puts us down or belittles us in any way, it is because of their own lack of self-esteem and is *not our problem.*

However, if we feel bad about ourselves, we may take the put-downs on board and let them diminish our confidence even more.

If we feel confident we shrug off the put-downs with the thought, 'He must be having a bad day'. We recognise that when old Sid has had a difficult meeting with his boss, he takes it out on us and *we don't take it personally.*

When we are confident and feel a sense of self-worth, we are never rude or sarcastic or unkind. We don't have to be. When we feel OK, we can afford to be gentle and patient with people and to accept their faults.

If someone is saying nasty things, it comes from the hurting space inside them. In fact *they are talking to themselves* but they project it out onto other people instead.

When we recognise this, we can listen to what people say and know that they are talking to an unacceptable part of themselves when they are telling others off or putting them down. It helps us to separate what belongs to us and what is their problem.

If someone makes us feel bad, we've taken something on board. Clearly they have plugged into a negative belief we hold about ourselves. So stop blaming them. It is time to look at ourselves. Maybe they have reminded us that we believe we are stupid, lazy, unworthy, unkind, dishonest or a failure. It could be any of a million negative beliefs we hold.

Our task is to isolate the negative beliefs and then start building positive beliefs into our unconscious mind. So if we feel bad in a certain situation we should ask ourselves what our underlying belief is. Perhaps we feel incapable. Then we affirm that we are capable and remind ourselves

of times we have done something capably. Preferably we write these times down to anchor them into our unconscious.

When we feel capable again, then we feel confident in that situation or with that person.

1 *Write a list* of things you are good at:

_____

2 What colour makes you feel confident? Picture a strong powerful aura of this colour around you. Keep reinforcing this in your imagination. Then imagine that you are bigger and entitled to more space. Wherever you are, sense yourself bigger than you really are and notice how people respond to the energy you are now transmitting.

Record your observations:

_____

3a Walk round imagining that the roof of your mouth is closer to the ground than it is to the ceiling. Notice how you feel. Observe your mood. Notice how you respond to other people.

_____

b Now walk round imagining that the roof of your mouth is closer to the ceiling than it is to the ground. Notice how you feel. Observe your mood. How do you respond to other people?

Most people feel much lighter, happier and more confident when they walk round as in **b**. Practise this constantly. The set of your body affects the perceptions of your mind.

Record your observations:

_____

Being lovable

The universal energy is Love. When our hearts are open, we flow with this unconditional Universal Love. Then we know we are completely lovable. We are also totally loving.

However, few of us are as enlightened and attuned as this. Most of us believe that we are not really lovable.

This means that if someone rejects us or abandons us or says something hurtful, we put up a wall to protect ourselves.

The more unlovable we believe we are, the more things we interpret as rejection, and the thicker the wall we put up to protect our vulnerable inner selves. Each time we interpret something as rejection, we add a brick to our defensive wall and move further away from other people.

If we are two years old and our parents quarrel or are distant with each other, we feel we must be unlovable or they wouldn't behave like this. We are terrified that, because we are clearly unlovable, they won't want us and we will be rejected or abandoned. It is too painful to feel our hurt and terror, so we partially close our hearts.

Hurt is unforgiveness. This pain continues to reverberate within us and affect us spiritually, physically and emotionally until we forgive. Forgiveness heals pain.

The two-year-old who is enlightened and connected to the ultimate source, which is love, knows that he is completely lovable. He knows that he is a loving spirit who has come into a body for this experience on earth. If his parents quarrel, he knows that it is their problem. He realises he is still lovable and that they each love him. They simply have a problem with loving each other.

Because he feels lovable, he knows he is safe and will never be rejected or abandoned. He trusts. He feels no pain. There is nothing to forgive.

He remains open and loving in all his relationships and, of course, everyone responds by loving him and treating him well.

The person who believes he is unlovable behaves in an unlovable way. For instance, he may be distant, offhand, rude or uncaring. Because he behaves like this, people treat him badly. He doesn't have to do or say anything. He simply sends out unlovable vibrations, which people pick up and respond to negatively.

And when we believe we are lovable, we are open and warm and caring and send out loving vibrations which people respond to. Others feel safe around us and they open up too. As we open our hearts and radiate love, we start a chain of love that spreads all around us.

1 If you believed you were really lovable, how differently would you behave and how would you respond to other people?

_____

_____

2 How much of this do you dare to put in action NOW, this minute?

_____

_____

3 Keep affirming, 'I love everyone and everyone loves me.' *Write this affirmation* several times.

_____

_____

4 Act as if you were really lovable and notice how it feels. *Record your feelings*:

_____

_____

Visualisation to open your heart

You may like to record this visualisation on to a tape or ask a friend to read it to you.

Find a quiet time when you will be undisturbed. If you would like to put on some gentle music please do so. This is your space.

Sit or lie comfortably with your spine straight. Then close your eyes and breathe rhythmically in a relaxed way. Take a few moments to focus on your feet to relax them, then your ankles, calves, knees, thighs, hips, tummy, solar plexus, chest, shoulders, arms, hands, lower back and up the spine, back of neck, back of head, face, forehead and scalp.

Place the palm of one of your hands on the centre of your chest. Think for a few moments of who you really are – not the little you in this body on the Earth – but the vast you who has lived for many lifetimes. You are an incredible being filled with knowledge and wisdom. Start to imagine the true beauty of your soul.

Sense a golden ball under the palm of your hand. Let it become soft and warm. You may even feel it tingle. The ball is pure love and is always inside you, in the calm, still space within your heart centre. Focus on this golden ball. Breathe into it. Allow it to grow bigger.

Feel love flowing out of your heart, linking you to everyone and everything.

Now think about the last time you felt hurt. See or sense yourself. This is your personality self; the part of you that is afraid, that has an ego.

Be aware of the wall you put around yourself to defend yourself from being hurt again. Notice the size, colour and texture of this wall. What is it made of?

Let the vast golden you, with your heart open, start to take down the wall round the hurting you.

When the wall is down, let your Higher Self, the golden

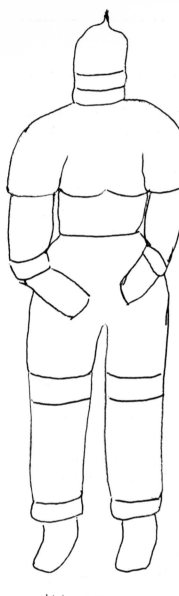

It's difficult
to make love
in armour

part of you, remind the personality self of all your lovable qualities and all the loving things people have done for you or said to you. Really take your time to recall beautiful, loving moments, kindnesses you have done to others or received, as well as times of strength or patience in your life.

Remember, love is stronger than fear. Light dissolves all darkness.

1 *Record* what you experienced during your visualisation:

_____

_____

2 *Write down* all the loving things you have done for people:

_____

_____

3 *Write down* all the loving things people have said to you or done for you:

_____

_____

The 'As If' principle

When we take a deep breath, imagine we are confident and act as if we really are confident, this impresses confidence on to our unconscious mind. So our inner computer receives confidence messages from us. It also registers the responses of other people towards us when we are acting confidently. This too is absorbed unconsciously as positive feedback.

So by acting as if we are confident, we make positive steps towards becoming confident.

A similar thing happens when we act as if we are lovable. We feel better and so people respond to us differently. This positive feedback makes the unconscious mind begin to take in the belief that we are lovable. Then it provides us with information which helps us to act as if we are lovable. Thus we become lovable.

Years ago I read about a group of students who decided to play a trick on a girl who was unattractive and not particularly friendly. They decided to treat her as if she was the most popular girl in the class. A quite extraordinary thing happened. By the end of the term she *was* the most popular girl in the class.

So the 'As If' principle also works on other people. We can treat people as if they are honest, clever, interesting, valuable, successful . . . and watch the effect. When we do this with integrity, enthusiasm and focus, it creates miracles.

In one workshop I was running I asked the participants to imagine each member of their family as an animal. Then they took a sheet of paper and drew these animals.

Because the unconscious mind knows things that we aren't consciously aware of, all sorts of interesting insights come up.

One lady had drawn most of her family at the bottom of the page. She found she had depicted herself and her brother-in-law, whom she disliked intensely, as birds on a branch above the family. She was an eagle and he was an owl.

When she got home after the workshop she thought a lot about that picture. She realised that consciously she disliked and despised her brother-in-law. Yet unconsciously she had placed him by her side, as a wise owl, watching over the family.

That afternoon her daughter's car broke down. Neither she nor her daughter knew anything about cars. Suddenly it came to her to ask the wise owl for advice. Until that time she would never have thought of asking him for help. She rang him. He was incredibly helpful.

From that moment she treated him as a wise person and the family dynamics changed. He became her ally, her supporter and defender within the family. He became a source of advice and help to her.

Because she treated him as wise, he responded by being wise.

1 What qualities do you want to enhance in your life? For instance, do you want to be more confident, joyful, dependable, friendly, have more fun? *I want to be more*:

_____

_____

2 Close your eyes and imagine yourself acting in this new way. Notice how this new behaviour feels. In what ways are you ready to put the 'As If' principle into operation in your life now? *Record your intention*:

_____

_____

3 If your family/people at work/friends were animals, what would they be? *Draw them* as animals and trust your unconscious mind to give you insights about them.

How we create our lives

Life on Earth is a school and we are all here learning lessons. We get tested from time to time on these lessons and the tests come in the form of difficulties, challenges, problems, awkward people and situations.

Every single thing or person in our life is there for a purpose. We choose, attract or create everything.

How is it that we choose certain difficulties? The Law of Karma ensures that as we give so we receive. Ultimately there is total justice which may take several lifetimes to work through.

This means that at a soul level, before we come into this life, we decide to deal with unresolved issues from other lives. Simplistically, if we have done something bad we will choose to have that same bad thing done to us or pay for it in some way. Equally, if we have done something good, the good will come back.

For our ultimate soul growth, we choose our parents, our family, our place and time of birth, our genetic inheritance. Many of our relationships will be pre-life choices.

How do we attract things and people into our lives? Our thoughts are magnets attracting what we think to us. Our thoughts come from our beliefs, so if we find we are magnetising things that we don't want in our lives, it is time to examine our beliefs.

If, for instance, we believe that it is a big bad world out there, we will be thinking unsafe thoughts. Our thoughts will be of insecurity, danger, attack or lack of trust. We will attract nasty people and situations into our lives, which will verify our beliefs.

If we know it is a beautiful, safe world, full of nice, kind, helpful people, we will attract that sort of person and will always be safe and looked after. This also confirms us in our original belief.

When we are totally in harmony with what we are doing, then we attract harmonious people and situations towards us.

How do we create things? We create things by focusing on them. Eventually whatever we focus on must materialise. So if we focus on failure, we make such a picture of failure in our minds that it materialises. The more energy we put into our gloomy picture of failure, the more quickly and surely it happens.

Similarly, when we focus on a positive vision it must take place. The only way we can stop our positive vision from manifesting is by sending out negative thoughts which block it.

The more power and energy we put into our vision, the more quickly it takes place.

1 What have you attracted or created in your life that you want to change? For instance, perhaps you have too little money, an unsatisfactory partner, a boring job? *List the things you want to change*:

_____

_____

2 Watch your thoughts on these subjects and *note them down*. Now you are aware, you can start to change them.

_____

_____

3 *Write a list* of people you like to be with and things you like to do that make you feel in harmony. How can you bring more of this harmony into your life?

_____

_____

Taking responsibility

When we accept that we choose, attract or create everything, then we are ready to take full responsibility for our lives. While we are poor little victims, believing we are pawns in the hands of fate or other people, we are stuck.

Everything and everyone in our lives is there because we have by our energy invoked it in to learn from. When we take responsibility, we gain mastery and then we can change things.

So when we have an accident, even if it appears to be someone else's fault, we need to take responsibility for the fact that *at some level* we invited it into our lives. Then we ask ourselves how we did that. Was the accident magnetised to our anger? Or to our fear? Which of our beliefs attracted the accident? Were we refusing to listen to what our body was telling us until it refused to function properly? If we didn't listen, why not?

Everything happens in accordance with Spiritual Law. No illness, injury, fire, burglary, promotion, redundancy or anything whatsoever occurs by chance.

At a soul level, no one can do anything to us, even murder us, without the agreement of our Higher Self.

If we are burgled, the sort of questions we can start asking ourselves are:

'Do I believe in loss or violation?'

'Am I holding on to things that it's time I let go of?'

'Am I hoarding things instead of sharing them?'

'Do I take things, possibly even emotionally, from others?'

'Is it time to replace old ideas, as well as things, with new ones?'

Many people have attracted redundancy, sometimes repeatedly if they won't listen, to show them it is time to move in a new direction. Redundancy is a major test. What are we meant to be learning? It is more sensible to learn what we need to learn than to moan and grumble and wait for the lesson to come again.

Fires always indicate anger. There is an inflamed situation to be looked at. Burns, scalds, inflammations all indicate anger. If we won't face up to

our anger, the Universe has a way of drawing it to our attention!

Gaining mastery means that we take responsibility for what we do unconsciously as well as for what we do consciously. Nothing we do is ever totally unintentional. If we say something hurtful, it is no use saying, 'I didn't mean to say that.' At some level we meant to say it. If we forget something, part of us intended to forget.

This doesn't mean that we blame ourselves. Quite the reverse. We accept responsibility and start to explore our unconscious reasons. Then we become conscious, enlightened beings.

1 Over the past two years what negative situations and people have you attracted into your life?

_____

_____

2 How were you out of harmony at the time?

_____

_____

3 Give yourself time and space to relax and be in harmony. Visualise harmonious things and people coming into your life.
   Record your impressions:

_____

_____

Affirmations

I'm happy and free
I enjoy being me

One of the most effective ways to replace old negative beliefs with new positive ones is to make daily affirmations.

An affirmation is a positive statement about ourselves or our abilities. Once impressed on the unconscious mind, the new positive statement becomes part of our belief system.

We put thousands of negative thoughts into our minds during our lifetime and we need to flood our minds with new positive affirmations in order to wash out the old ones.

Affirmations must be in the present tense. Our unconscious mind is a computer which has no concept of time, and therefore tomorrow never comes. So our statement does not say: 'I will be healthy.' It affirms: 'I am healthy.'

It is important that our affirmations contain only positive words, so don't say: 'I let go of fear.' Fear is negative and focuses our minds on fear. Instead, put it positively: 'I now have courage.'

Our computer can't deal with 'not'. If we tell ourselves that we don't want to imagine a car the only thing we can picture is a car! If we affirm that we don't want chocolate, the computer disregards 'don't' and focuses on chocolate and we then crave it. Again, put the affirmation in positive terms, such as: 'I desire healthy foods.' 'I love crunchy salads.'

In order to get into the unconscious mind the affirmation must slip past the critical censor of the mind. Long cumbersome affirmations alert the critical censor which wakes up and rejects them.

Rhythm and rhyme help lull the censor so that affirmations can flow into the unconscious. My book *A Time for Transformation* contains many rhyming affirmations. Here are a few:

**Love flows through every cell
So I am healthy and well.**

**Centred and in harmony
I attract good things to me.**

**I'm safe and secure,
Guided and sure.**

They all flow and they all contain positive words only. If you can't make up rhyming affirmations, make up short clear ones.

Remember the 'As If' principle. When we make our affirmations, we start to act as if we already have these qualities.

When we change our beliefs to positive ones, we can only attract good and wonderful things into our lives. When we are in harmony, we are magnets for harmonious conditions.

1 Which areas of your life do you want to improve – relationships, sex, money, learning ability, confidence . . . ?
   List them:

_____

_____

2 *Write affirmations* using the principles described:

_____

_____

The inner child

The pleaser

The deep core of each of us is very vulnerable. It is as if we have a vulnerable child within us who is too small to look after himself. He craves to be loved and cared for. To defend this vulnerable little child within us, we develop other child personalities in an effort to keep him safe. The first personality we develop is the pleaser.

As a small baby our food and emotional nourishment come from our mother and our very survival depends on keeping her loving us. To do this we believe we have to please her. We soon learn that she responds when we smile. While we are happy to smile that's fine. We are genuine. But if we see that she's miserable and we feel threatened, we look for a way to coax her to be happy and loving. We remember that she responds when we smile, so we smile when we don't really feel like it. This is when our false pleaser is born.

We have given our power away because we have to please people to keep them liking us. When we are powerless we feel angry, resentful or hurt and we hide our feelings. And because our very survival depends on pleasing, we bury the hurt and anger and learn to deny it. Unconsciously we prefer to be fat or to have tummyache, cancer, arthritis or one of the other diseases caused by buried feelings, rather than risk rejection.

Whenever we try to please someone instead of being genuine, we are being dishonest. People sense that we are artificial and don't entirely trust us. They certainly don't value or respect us. In our desire to please we can easily be taken for granted or become martyrs.

When we are pleasers we don't value ourselves, so we turn our anger inward. And our pleaser will make us feel guilty if we are not nice because its job is to keep us loved at any cost. We bury our neediness. Often we crave to be nurtured, but we deny this need and devote ourselves to caring for others.

We know when our pleaser is balanced and honest because we feel valued and respected. We are genuinely charming, friendly and surrounded by friends, and we are healthy and happy.

The rebel

If pleasing doesn't work ... if, however hard we try, we can't seem to be lovable enough ... if we don't get enough attention, though we try to do the right thing, then we may become a rebel. We may also rebel if we have a controlling parent.

It may seem that the only way to get our needs met is to challenge our parents. We'll probably get into trouble but it does get us noticed. Sometimes people are frightened of us, which is our way of controlling. We create problems or excitement which mask our hurt feelings.

1 In what way do you please others? What or who makes you feel guilty? *Make a list*:

_____

2 What do you really want to do? Start with small things and then *list* the more important things:

_____

3 *Tick each item on your list* as you do it. Remember, no one else can make you feel bad unless you let them.

4 What do you use to keep your anger down? Food, sweets, cigarettes, alcohol? Something else? Against each thing *write something appropriate* you could do instead, e.g. talk honestly to the other person, exercise, deep breathing.

_____

Visualisation *to heal the inner child*

You may like to record this visualisation on to a tape or ask a friend to read it to you.

Close your eyes and make yourself comfortable. Breathe easily. Then start at your toes and imagine each part of your body becoming soothed and relaxed.

You are now ready to allow your unconscious mind to start healing the child within you, who had to please to survive. You can allow your inner child to reclaim its power.

See or sense yourself going into a house and walking up to a door which leads down to the cellar. Open this door. If it is dark put on the light. It is quite safe, but if you wish you may take someone with you.

Walk down the steps into the cellar. You are seeking the small child within you who felt so vulnerable that it had to give away its power by pleasing others or rebelling.

Find the little child. Sense how old he is. Put your arms round him and hold him. Reassure him. Promise him that you will never abandon him again. You are now able to help him in a way you couldn't when you were small.

Pick him up and carry him up the steps into the light. Help your child to stand up for himself in a pleasant, friendly but firm way. Teach him that he can say 'No' and you will support him.

Give your child permission to do all the things he wants to do. What are your child's gifts and talents? Encourage them all, however small, and watch your child glow and gain confidence.

Have fun with your child. Take time to do things together that you really enjoy doing.

Promise your child that you will always try to

understand him and encourage him. Then put him into your heart.

And now find creative solutions for all your current problems. Then you can imagine your adult self doing the things you want to do and enjoying them.

As you do what pleases you, be aware of the respect others have for the new, stronger you.

Record what you experienced during your visualisation:

_____

_____

The driver

If we feel confident as children, then we are happy to try new things and we enjoy doing our best. Because we are relaxed and expect to succeed, we do well. When we do well it makes our parents happy, so they give us the praise, warmth and attention we need. This in turn increases our confidence. And we become adults who can balance work and play. In healthy competition, we match ourselves against others to sharpen our skills and have fun. If we don't win, it doesn't dent our confidence.

But one of the beliefs most commonly held by our inner child is that we aren't good enough. This belief reduces our confidence and self-esteem. To the extent that we feel this, we have to prove ourselves to our parents. This means we have to justify ourselves by doing well, so that they won't reject us.

This is when we develop an inner driver who constantly strives to do well. This child strives relentlessly to succeed at school so that our parents will praise us. He drives us to do as well as or better than our siblings or classmates. If we fail in a competition our unhealthy driver feels terrible and relives every moment of defeat because it confirms his suspicion that he isn't good enough. To our inner driver, defeat is rejection.

Inside every over-stressed adult or workaholic there is an unbalanced inner child driving us to work harder to prove to our parents, who may have died long ago, that we are good enough.

The lazy layabout

If we try our best to prove ourselves to Mum or Dad and we still don't get the validation or attention we need, then we may make an unconscious choice to give up. It may be that a sibling or parent is cleverer than we are and however hard we try we can't match up to them. It may be that our family is critical or indifferent to our efforts. It may be that our family is achievement-oriented and the only thing that merits interest or praise is doing well. If our inner child believes that however hard he tries, he can never get what he needs from his parents, he simply stops trying.

To the outer world such a person may seem lazy and be called a

layabout. He may drop out of school or work because he doesn't think he'll ever be good enough to succeed. When this person says he's bored, he is saying, 'I don't want to try because I'm afraid I won't succeed'. Many of us use the excuse of boredom to hide our feelings of inadequacy.

This child within us needs a great deal of encouragement in order to regain his confidence step by step in manageable stages. We chose our family circumstances so we can't blame them or expect them to change. Instead we need to start a programme of constant self-encouragement to regain our confidence. Then we can succeed at anything we want.

1 *Identifying the driver/lazy child*:

Do you become stressed about work?_____

Do you have to be perfect?_____

Are you bored?_____

Are you lazy?_____

Do you give up easily?_____

2 Remember, your parents could only do to you what was done to them. When they talked to you, they were really talking to themselves. You are continuing to do this to yourself. You selectively choose to hear, see and interpret according to your preconceived programming.

As a child, what messages did you take in about being good enough? e.g. 'You're no good with your hands.' 'Your brother is cleverer.'

_____

3 What does your inner child need in order to feel confident and who does he need this from?

_____

Find a space where you will be undisturbed. This is your time. You are important. You need some time for yourself.

You may like to record this visualisation on to a tape or ask a friend to read it to you.

Make yourself really nice and comfortable, with your spine straight and your feet on the floor. Close your eyes and relax your body by breathing slowly and deeply. Focus on any tension spots in your body and breathe out of those spots. Feel the tension dissolving away.

Imagine the last time you felt bored, stressed, inadequate or a failure. Picture what happened and what was said and then become aware of how your body is feeling.

See in front of you a door marked with your name. Notice the colour of the door and put your hand on the handle. Open the door and go through it. You will find steps taking you down.

As you walk down the steps you will notice that there are rooms off to each side. Glance into these rooms until you find the child who needs your help.

Hold, love and reassure your little child. Reassure him that you love him whether he succeeds or not.

Take time to remind him of all his gifts and good points. Encourage him to relax and try new things if he is afraid. Encourage him to relax as he does things. Remind him that you love him anyway. Give him permission to enjoy what he does rather than constantly striving. If he gives up too easily, firmly help him to try again. Make it fun.

One by one bring in the people you wanted validation

or recognition from as a child. Visualise these people giving your child the praise and encouragement and recognition he needs. See or sense your child becoming more confident. Take time to enjoy and experience the way this feels in your body.

Do this exercise frequently until you feel more relaxed and confident.

Record what you experienced during your visualisation:

_____

_____

The inner child (continued)

The victim and the rescuer

To protect our vulnerable inner child, many of us develop a victim personality. Our victim sends out a message: 'Poor me. I can't cope. Please look after me.' This soon hooks in someone to rescue him and look after him, so it is a very powerful protection for his vulnerable inner child.

Because the victim is afraid to take responsibility for his own life, he feels hopeless and helpless. He feels like a pawn in the hands of fate and blames everyone else for what is happening to him. So he blames his childhood, his parents, the education system or the state for his situation. He blames his lack of success on his bad boss or ill-health. He is convinced everything that happens around him is someone else's fault. 'Poor me. I'm so unlucky,' he whinges. He is determined to stay stuck because he believes that he can't look after himself. If he admits responsibility for his life, who will take care of his vulnerable child? So if someone tries to help him, he finds a million reasons why he can't do anything. 'Yes . . . but' and 'can't' are his stock phrases.

For everyone who is a victim, there is a rescuer keeping him stuck. A rescuer is a victim in disguise. The rescuer would rather look at someone else's problems than his own. It gives him an illusion of being in control of his life and he feels useful and needed without having to admit that there is anything wrong.

The rescuer tells the victim he's unlucky, there's nothing that can be done. He agrees with his victim that it is all someone else's fault. He supports him in his belief that he can't manage alone. He does things for him instead of teaching him to do things for himself.

The rescuer disempowers people. He has nothing to gain from helping the victim to take responsibility for himself and stand alone. He wouldn't be needed any more. When we think someone can't manage without us, whether it is a client, a relative or a friend, we need to look at the rescuer inside us.

The victim and the rescuer have a contract, a collusion, which they play out together. This is: 'I'll look after you as long as you agree to

need me and depend on me.' Occasionally the victim, like the worm, can turn and persecute the rescuer. Then the rescuer is exposed and feels terribly upset and betrayed.

There is a little victim in most of us. Few of us take full responsibility for our conscious and unconscious actions. The victim says such things as: 'I forgot,' 'I didn't mean it,' or 'You hurt me.' He says: 'Everything would be fine if only I didn't have insomnia or if only he loved me.'

When we gain mastery we take responsibility for choosing our feelings. When something happens we say: 'This has happened. I am responsible. How have I created it? Now I can change it.' Every single time we take responsibility, we empower ourselves and take a step towards mastery.

1 Who or what do you blame for making you feel bad?

_____

_____

2 Now accept responsibility for choosing your feelings, your attitude and for creating the situation. How can you change your attitude or what you say or do to create something different? (Remember, people pick up what you think as if you have said it and respond accordingly.) For example, 'I accept I meant to hurt you. I wanted to punish you for devaluing me.' Start valuing yourself and *write down* some affirmations of self-worth:

_____

_____

The rationaliser

Sometimes as small children we receive conflicting messages from our parents. Perhaps our mother is warm one moment and cool the next. We feel confused and uncertain.

Perhaps our parents say one thing but as a sensitive child we sense that something different is going on. A common example of this is when the parents declare, 'Of course Mummy and Daddy love each other.' When they are denying the reality that their relationship is in conflict, we sense this and our feelings of reality are undermined.

There are families where all the emotions hang out. Everything is over the top. As children we find this too overwhelming to cope with.

In order to make sense of the chaos and confusion around us, we may go into our heads and think everything through. It is our only way of being in control of the situation. We have to rationalise, to intellectualise everything, in order to survive the confusion.

When we choose this defence mechanism we develop our left brain and don't want to know about emotions.

If as a child we undergo a trauma, hurt or problem which is never acknowledged or worked through, we have to bury the feelings. This means a part of us remains emotionally stuck at the age of the trauma. We may be very intellectual but we daren't feel.

Many of us get the message that feelings are unacceptable. We are told or it is inferred that boys must be strong and brave and never cry. As girls we pick up that it isn't ladylike to be angry or stand up for ourselves.

In some families whole areas of emotion are denied. In some it is anger, in others it is hurt or sadness or fear or pain or grief or sexuality. Because we believe it is unacceptable to express these feelings, we hold on to them. They may be trapped in our tummy or back or eyes or any part of our body.

When we are adults, our inner child will sense these same denied emotions in others. It may remind us by giving us tummyache, backache, eye pain or whatever, or in extreme cases we may totally block our physical

I don't feel anything.
I'm in control

sensations. We may not feel cold or hunger or pain. We are busy rationalising it all and then we find we can't cope with angry or emotional people. Of course not; our inner child can't cope, so we go into our heads to escape the feelings.

In this case we may be patronising, unaware or insensitive. We may speak in slow and measured tones to get control of the chaos. We may attract a partner who carries the emotions for both of us. More often we'll attract a partner who denies exactly the same emotions as we do. *However, we will inevitably draw into our lives people who display the emotions we deny* because our Higher Self is giving us opportunities to heal our inner child.

Our thinker protects us from feeling emotions. Remember, we can't deny the pain in life without also denying the joy.

1 What feelings do you feel? For instance, do you allow yourself to feel happiness, grief, excitement, pain?

_____

_____

2 What feelings do you deny? When were you last angry, hurt, joyous, sad?

_____

_____

3 Review your life and decide what feelings would have been appropriate in the different circumstances you have experienced.

_____

_____

Visualisation to release your child's feelings

Find a quiet space for yourself where you will not be disturbed. As with the other visualisations you may like to record this on to a tape or ask a friend to read it to you.

Close your eyes. Start with your toes and tense them up, then relax them. Do the same with your feet, ankles, calves, knees, thighs. Then tense and relax both your legs. You may find it helps to shake them a little now. Continue to tense and relax your pelvis, abdomen, stomach, hands, arms and shoulders. Give your arms and shoulders a shake and shrug. Tighten your throat and relax it. Tighten your mouth and then open it wide. Close your eyes tight and then open them wide. Now you can let yourself breathe deeply and relax.

Visualise yourself going into a beautiful garden. Imagine what it would be like to smell the flowers, to feel the warm sun on your body and to hear the birds singing. There is a gate at the end of the garden. Open it and go through it. In the garden you find yourself as a small child.

Your child is very vulnerable and has blocked off his feelings. As you approach him, sense what these feelings are. He cannot tell you until he feels he can trust you. What does he need from you in order to trust you? Gently, patiently and lovingly reassure him that you are here to help him and that you will never leave him again. Befriend him until he feels safe with you and trusts you to look after him. It may take a long time but you can have as long as you like in this inner time space. Even if he needs a whole lifetime of love and understanding, you can give it to him now.

When he trusts you, let him talk. Listen to what he has to tell you and acknowledge what a difficult experience it was for him.

Explain to him that you understand it was too difficult or dangerous then to express what he felt. Now you are

looking after him, so it is safe. Encourage him to express what he needs to.

You may visualise him giving vent to his feelings or you may become the child and beat a cushion or cry or shake with fear. When he has finished, hug him and praise him for expressing the feelings.

You can hear your mother calling you. How does this sound and how does your child feel? What happens when they meet? Encourage your child to express whatever he genuinely feels inside, not what he rationally thinks. No one can harm your child while you are there to look after him and he no longer has to protect his mother's feelings.

Now you can hear your father calling you. How does this sound and how does your child feel? Let them meet and experience what it is like. Now you can help your child to express honestly and fearlessly what he wants to. You can protect him and no one can hurt him while you look after him, nor does he need to protect his father's feelings.

Let the sun come out and fill your inner scene with light as you hug your child. Hold his hand as you bring him out into the beautiful garden again.

Write or draw what you experienced during your visualisation:

_____

_____

The inner child (continued)

The manipulator

In order to help our vulnerable inner child survive, we have to get enough love or some sort of substitute for love. A child who doesn't receive any love dies and if we can't get our basic needs met by being open and honest, we will manipulate things to get them met.

Again, no one is born into a totally open, honest, loving family. All families are disfunctional. After all, life on Earth is a school and we wouldn't need to go to school if we knew it all.

As we pinpoint the manipulations of our inner child, we can gently start the task of changing our behaviours and attitudes into open, honest, direct, loving ones.

Many of us use food to manipulate others. Being difficult about food is calculated to get masses of concerned attention from the average mother. So, to get attention, our inner child may make us go off food, be very fussy, eat slowly or very quickly. We may eat noisily or messily which gets us frowned at.

Our little child may have controlled Mum by dressing slowly or untidily, or by being untidy. This sort of behaviour got us attention. Our inner manipulator may carry the dressing slowly scenario into being unpunctual as an adult. By being late we are still trying to control our parents.

When we couldn't ask openly for attention, our inner manipulator may have quite unconsciously used illness to get it. What better than tummyache, headache, asthma or tiredness to keep us off school or to keep Mummy caring for us? And of course our unconscious mind is so powerful, we would have created a genuine painful headache or streaming cold. Many of us still use illness as a manipulation to deal with adult life.

Anger and tantrums are common manipulations. We may make a scene because we feel it is the only way to be heard. Many of us cry or sulk or become withdrawn or touchy to get our own way.

One way of getting power is to set people very subtly against each other. When we tell lies or exaggerate, our manipulator is at work; as he is when we deliberately say things to confuse others or say 'Yes' when we mean 'No'.

Instead of telling our sister what we want her to hear, we may tell our brother instead, knowing it will get back to our sister. An extension of this is asking someone else to tell our sister on our behalf. There is also a touch of the little victim at work here. Poor me, she takes no notice when I tell her.

Threats of suicide or blackmail or of hurting someone are the ultimate manipulations.

Where we find our manipulator, we need to practise claiming our power by being open and direct.

1 In what ways do you manipulate? And what is it that you really want?

_____

_____

2 How could you get your needs met honestly, clearly and directly?

_____

_____

3 Practise doing this and *record* what you do and how it feels:

_____

_____

The hurt child

If we feel we have tried everything to make ourself safe and loved but none of it works, then we put a big solid wall round ourselves to protect our hurt, vulnerable child.

Our hurt child expects to be abused emotionally or physically. So naturally we attract abuse.

Because we expect rejection we protect ourselves by not reaching out. We may become withdrawn, depressed or isolated. Or we may keep others away from us by being rude, sarcastic, difficult or cruel.

We expect others to attack us and we become paranoid or suspicious.

Our pain is too intense to bear so we shut down our feelings. This means that we can't feel other people's feelings either. We become insensitive or hard or hurtful or cruel. The child who pulls a cat's tail has switched off from his feelings so that he doesn't feel the cat's pain. No open, sensitive, feeling child could do this.

Terrible acts of cruelty are always perpetrated by someone with a very hurt inner child.

We all switch off from our feelings from time to time. It is a survival mechanism. If our inner child is excessively hurt, we may become schizophrenic or even psychotic.

A very hurt child may, alternatively, become totally overbearing and tyrannical.

We nearly all have a hurt child somewhere inside us and we need to listen to his needs. If no one was there to hear our needs in childhood, it is up to us now to do this for ourselves.

If we find ourselves being rude, stubborn, sarcastic, hurtful or unkind, we should ask ourselves what part of us feels so vulnerable that we need to protect ourselves in this way. What is our fear and how can we help our inner child?

We must be gentle in healing our hurt inner child, for he is very fragile. We wouldn't beat a baby who was unhappy. We would listen to what it was trying to communicate and we would meet its needs.

And our hurt child also needs to be heard and understood. Then he needs support, encouragement and love.

We chose our parents knowing how they would treat us. We unconsciously treat our children as we were treated and they become hurt in their turn. As we heal ourselves, we heal our children and it is the greatest gift we can give them.

It is time now to come out from behind our walls and open our hearts so that we can heal our hurt inner child.

1 Notice when you are touchy, insensitive, oversensitive, rude, sarcastic, overbearing, demanding, suspicious, paranoid or defensive in any other way. *Write down* what you discover:

_____

_____

2 What do you need in order to feel safe enough to dissolve your defences?

_____

_____

3a Visualise yourself receiving what you need.

 b Start acting in an open, undefensive way.
    Note what happens:

_____

_____

Empowering the playful, creative child

If we didn't feel safe as children, we couldn't truly play and be curious and explore.

We may not have felt safe because we were emotionally confused or still excessively attached to Mum. We may have been traumatised. We may have had a very nervous parent or one who was critical or authoritarian. Our efforts may have been ridiculed or ignored so that our initiative was stamped on, or we may have been over-praised.

If our parents were never able to play or create or fantasize, how could they encourage us to do so? If we in turn were shouted down when we were noisy, told not to make a mess, not to get dirty, not to be untidy, not to hurt ourselves or not to have silly ideas, our joy and creativity will have been stultified.

If our child has never learnt to play, our adult self can't let go and have fun. If our child never danced or sang or painted, how can we be creative? If our child wasn't allowed to examine, explore and satisfy his curiosity, how can we open up to the magical, fantastic world of opportunity?

Some people find it helpful literally to do all the things they were prevented from doing as children – experimenting with playdoh, making mud pies and sandcastles, getting wet and dirty, jumping in puddles, playing with sand, clay, plasticine, painting with finger paints, colouring with crayons and experiencing how it feels. Or climbing a tree, singing and chanting, playing drums or a musical instrument, intuitively not formally.

The more we cringe at these suggestions, the more our inner child needs to be liberated! The sense of fun and freedom is often enhanced when we do it with a friend or friends.

If our inner child is out of balance the other way and feels unbounded, unstructured and confused, we may become an adult who has wild orgies, dabbles in black magic, abuses drugs and alcohol or lives in a fantasy world. We will lose touch with the reality of deep inner joy.

Both the inhibited inner child and the unbounded one need safety, *appropriate* encouragement and empowerment. When our inner child is free to be playful and creative we can:

enjoy ourselves without alcohol or drugs

sing without inhibition

move our bodies freely and expressively

paint creatively whether we're talented or not

be curious and interested in everything

constantly create and invent new things

be intensely alive and have fun

feel safe trying new things

be gloriously happy and healthy.

1 What did you enjoy doing as a child or what would you have liked to do if you had dared, e.g. writing stories or poetry, drawing, dancing, acting, singing nursery rhymes, telling jokes, plasticine modelling, making model aeroplanes, playing the recorder, climbing trees? *Record it*, however trivial:

_____

2 If you felt totally confident in yourself and your ability, what would you like to do or create now?

_____

3 How can you develop these skills? What can you try now? They are latent within you, waiting to be developed.

_____

Visualisation for the creative child

Find a space where you can be comfortable and undisturbed. This is a way of nourishing yourself and is important for your wellbeing.

You may like to record this on to a tape or ask a friend to read it to you.

Close your eyes and breathe deeply. Focus on each part of your body in turn and as you breathe out allow your breath to stroke that part of your body until you are totally relaxed.

Find yourself walking down a road on a journey back into your childhood. You are now a strong and confident adult coming back to free and empower your child with enriching experiences. Ahead of you is a house where you lived as a child. Go up to the front door and open it. Walk through the house until you find yourself as a child.

Don't be surprised if your child is afraid or withdrawn. He has been waiting here for a long time. Take his hand and tell him you will be looking after him from now on. Explain that he doesn't need to worry about displeasing anyone because you are now going to care for him totally. Reassure him until he feels safe.

When your child feels safe, and trusts you, ask him what he wants to do to have fun. Tell him you have enough time to do everything, so he can do the small things as well as the large ones. If he wants to paint or draw let him have all the paints or crayons he wants. Let him have reams of paper and be free to experiment or create whatever he needs to. Laugh with him if he gets covered in paint. Remind him it washes off. If he wants to write, allow him quiet and space and encourage him appropriately.

He may want to play music. Let him. If he wants to dance, dance with him. If he wants to sing, listen to him, or sing with him. Enjoy it.

Was your child allowed to get muddy and wet? Was

he allowed to climb trees or to explore? Was he allowed to swim and play games? Was he allowed to cycle? You can take him to do all the things he was not able to do before. Let him explore and experience with your constructive help and guidance. Praise him and encourage him appropriately.

And now the two of you are going on a magical journey together. You can go to any part of the world and experience whatever adventure you want. If he would prefer it, take him out into the Universe to explore other planets or go together into mystic realms and meet fairies and mermaids and giants. Use your creative imagination to take you into your own wonderland where you can really enjoy yourselves.

Bring all this joyous creative energy back into your childhood home. Fill it with bright colours. Put your child in your heart and return down the road to the place where you live now.

Creatively visualise your adult self totally liberated and free to do what you want to do. Fill your current home with bright coloured light.

Write or draw what you experienced during your visualisation:

_____

_____

Healing our childhood

Whenever we have an over-the-top reaction to anything (in other words our response is excessive) we know we have something within us from our childhood that remains unhealed.

We record our impressions of our childhood on a kind of microfilm in the unconscious. However, because we filter the recording through our belief system, it may bear little resemblance to reality.

Little Johnny comes into this life with a belief that men with moustaches are cruel. His uncle, who is big, gruff and red-faced, has a moustache. Because of Johnny's belief about men with moustaches, he expects his uncle to do cruel things. Whatever his uncle does, he interprets as cruel.

When he sees his uncle in the kitchen holding a carving knife, he hides in a cupboard for two hours in absolute terror. It is indelibly marked in his unconscious mind that he is under threat of murder from his cruel uncle.

In adulthood he naturally attracts the people he fears, so he has a boss and a father-in-law with moustaches. When he is alone with them, he finds himself shaking with fear.

He needs to heal his childhood by closing his eyes and letting the memory of the original incident with his uncle surface. Then he can change the picture in the microfilm, perhaps by letting his parents come in and show him he's safe or by making friends with the uncle. Then this incident need no longer affect his adult life.

Of course, some of us may really have had a horrendous experience or a feeling of abandonment or not being loved in childhood. The same principle applies.

If we are reminded in some way of these experiences, we may feel sudden rage or terrible fear or total emptiness or some other overpowering emotion.

When one of these feelings strikes us, we need to focus on the feeling and let our minds float back to childhood. When we find the childhood experience or feeling, it is time to change it. We can throw our creative energy into changing the original picture in our unconscious.

As we practise this, there may well be times when an earlier picture from another life emerges. These pictures can be dealt with in a similar way.

1 When did you last have an over-the-top reaction, for instance, an inappropriately violent feeling of anger, hurt, grief, emptiness, jealousy or negative emotion?
   Describe your emotions and what happened:

   _____

   _____

2 *Note* other times when you have had an inappropriate emotional response:

   _____

   _____

3 *Write* a story or play about one of these times, with yourself as the main character. In the play, you respond in a totally different way to the emotional stimulus. Use your creative imagination and give your story an optimistic, happy ending.

   _____

   _____

Visualisation *to heal emotions*

Find a place where you can be quiet and undisturbed. If possible, light a candle and make this a special space.

You may like to record this visualisation on to a tape or ask a friend to read it to you.

Relax by looking at the candle for some time, then let your eyes close and continue to see the flame in your mind's eye for as long as you can. Breathe softly into your forehead all the while and allow your body to let go.

Recall the last time you had an over-the-top response to something or someone. Go over everything that happened just before you reacted, so hear what was said or remember what was done as vividly as possible. Let yourself relive the emotions that came up for you then.

Note where you are holding the emotions. How does your body feel? Does it feel hot, cold, stabbed, crushed, aching, bursting or something else?

How do you feel? For example, are you hurt, angry, empty, jealous, afraid or guilty?

Float back in your life to the time when you were a child and first experienced this feeling. How old are you now? What is happening for you as a child to arouse this feeling? It must have been very difficult for you.

Bring in someone who can give you the comfort that you needed then but couldn't get. It may be a parent, another adult, a religious figure or your adult self. Let this person talk to your inner child, so that he knows someone understands what a hard time he had. Let this person help him to feel safe and lovable and worthwhile. Take as long as you need until your child feels much better.

Now let the adult put a hand on your child's chest over his heart, radiating loving warmth to your child. Imagine his heart gently being filled with beautiful golden light until it opens like a flower.

The golden energy is radiating round him and

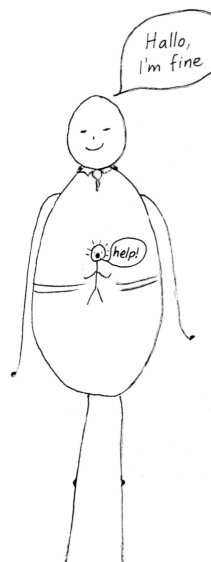

everyone is touched by it and loving him. When he looks and feels a safe, lovable, golden child, notice how everyone responds differently to him.

Now create a different scenario out of the original trauma.

Imagine something very positive and happy taking place instead. You are totally in charge now, so put as much emotional energy as you can into the new scene. Remember it is never too late to have a happy childhood and that your childhood affects your adult life.

Take your happy child back into your body.

Notice the warm feeling inside you as you open your eyes and look at the candle again.

The more often you do this and the more emotion you put into it, the more quickly you will be able to choose an appropriate response to this stimulus instead of reacting in an over-the-top way.

Record what you experienced during your visualisation:

_____

_____

Our parents

Whenever there is something unresolved from another life, we desire at a soul level to resolve it.

Most of us have all sorts of things to clear up in our relationships and so we reincarnate again and again with those same people until we have worked things through.

Our parents are no exception. We choose them because we have unresolved issues to deal with and they can teach us what we need to learn. It may be that we have to deal with rejection, so we choose a mother who is likely to reject us. (Most of us then bitterly blame our mother, instead of thanking her for the opportunity she has given us for growth!)

Souls who choose to be adopted have chosen to have one set of genetic parents and different parents to bring them up. Both are pre-life choices that have been made with the intention of learning lessons. It is often difficult to go through life with no blood relations close to us but we make the choice for our higher growth.

The type of mother and father we choose embody our challenge for this life.

If we have authoritarian parents, they will be very afraid of the big bad world out there. It is this fear which makes them so overbearing in their efforts to keep us safe.

If we perceive them as authoritarian, it is because we have the same belief in a bad, unsafe world. In this case we will become authoritarian ourselves. We will internalise the authoritarian energy so that we have an authoritarian voice in our heads which orders us about in an effort to keep us safe.

So we have chosen this parent with a specific challenge for our life. *Our challenge is to face our fears.*

Naturally, once we have learnt our lesson, we feel safe inside ourselves. We then attract a safe outer world. And either our parents change towards us or their attitude doesn't bother us any more.

A controlling parent fears chaos and confusion. They may fear abandonment and so they control us and others. *Our lesson is to stop controlling and to trust.*

A critical parent is very judgemental. When we internalise the critical parent voice, then we have a constant nagging self-criticism going on in our heads. It can drive us to depression or despair or suicide. *Our lesson is to accept and love ourselves.*

1 Is one of your parents authoritarian, controlling or critical? If so *write about* your parent and their fears:

_____

_____

2 In what way are you authoritarian, controlling or critical of others?

_____

_____

3 What does the voice in your head keep saying to you? How does it make you feel?

_____

_____

Visualisation to connect with your wise parents

Find a place where you can be quiet and undisturbed. Take the phone off the hook, tell everyone you want your own space and shut the door firmly.

You may like to record this visualisation on to a tape or ask a friend to read it to you.

Make yourself comfortable, with your spine straight and your feet flat on the floor.

Close your eyes and relax your body by breathing deeply for a few moments.

Focus on your feet and imagine them getting very heavy. Then imagine roots going down from your feet into the earth. These roots are grounding you and they are bringing up wonderful healing earth energy to help you. Take a little while to get the feeling of this.

Now imagine a golden cord going up from the base of your spine, up your back, through the crown of your head and then straight up into the air, until it links with your Higher Self. You may sense your Higher Self as a light or in any other way that comes to you. And now see the golden cord linking you to the Source, or Divine Intelligence. Take a little while to feel the wonder of this.

Imagine your inner parents coming into your scene. They represent the negative voices in your head which control you and they may look suspiciously like your real mother and father.

One or both of them may be angry, hurting, greedy, manipulative or jealous. They may be controlling, demanding, authoritarian or terrified of you getting hurt. These are all fears.

Ask your inner mother to sit down in front of you. Her fears are the reason why she talks to you as she does. Take time to listen to her fears. Respect what she says and thank her for doing her best to look after you. Tell her that

wise parents waiting

you are now an adult and are ready to take care of yourself in a new way. Ask her to leave your inner scene.

And now let your inner father sit in front of you and listen to what he is frightened of. He talks constantly to you as he does because he is afraid. Thank him for doing the best he could to look after you. Tell him that you are now ready to look after yourself in a new positive way and ask him to leave your inner scene.

Now bring in new, safe, wise parents who can give you freedom and encouragement.

What does your wise mother say to you? Listen to her wise advice. Hear her loving, encouraging words.

What does your wise father say to you? Listen to his advice and encouragement. Remember that he is fair and firm and will never allow anyone to hurt you or criticise you.

How do you feel as a result of this? How does this change your attitude? What changes can you make in your life?

When you are ready, open your eyes and return to the room, resolving to keep your connection with your wise parents.

Record what you experienced during your visualisation:

_____

_____

Choosing our parents

We choose partners who make us feel the same way as we did with our parents. This is because we are still trying to heal our childhood by getting from our partner what we couldn't get from our parents.

It is only when we stop trying to get our partner to meet our needs, and concentrate on meeting our own needs, that we start to accept our life's challenge.

Some souls choose a parent who is emotionally or physically distant or absent. *The challenge they have chosen for this life is to love themselves and be attentive to their own needs.*

If we chose an emotionally distant or physically absent parent, we will choose a partner who can't be there for us in some way. We may choose a married man or a person who is emotionally cold or someone who works away. This is because we are substituting them for Mummy or Daddy and trying to get them to be there for us. We have, of course, chosen someone with whom closeness is impossible. While we are on this quest, someone safe and present would be boring and possibly claustrophobic.

When we parent ourselves to meet our needs, then we can attract a close loving relationship.

If we have chosen a weak, wishy-washy, unsupportive parent, we are automatically going to have a vacillating, unhelpful, weak voice in our head. *Our challenge is to parent ourselves in a firm, encouraging, supportive way.* Then we become strong and can support ourselves and others.

If we have chosen a careless, uncaring parent, or one who is a hypochondriac, we are going to have to look after them in order to get our survival needs met. This means we in turn will become careless of our own needs. We too may resort to illness to get cared for or we will despise and ignore our bodily needs. *Our challenge is to nurture and care for ourselves.* Only then can we attract caring nurturing people into our lives.

If we have chosen aggressive, violent, cruel parents, we have chosen the ultimate lesson in learning to love ourselves. We may have chosen those parents for our growth, but at birth it was so terrifying that we walled ourselves off. Then they picked up our fear and battered us.

We will then become cruel to others in our turn and will most certainly be very cruel to ourselves.

Sometimes when we have chosen aggressive, violent, cruel parents, we have offered our soul in service to them and stayed loving enough to open a chink in their hearts. Then we become wise, loving healers.

1 What sort of parents did you have?

_____

2 *If our parents were:*   *our challenge is:*

If our parents were:	our challenge is:
authoritarian	to face our fears
controlling	to free ourselves
pushy	to achieve our potential
absent	to become independent
uncaring	to care for ourselves
critical	to approve of ourselves
all in their heads	to feel our feelings
over-emotional	to be disciplined
out of control	to be firm and realistic
weak and unsupportive	to be strong

The challenges I have chosen for this life are:

_____

3 What changes can you make so that you accept your challenges?

_____

Visualisation to find positive parents

Find a space where you can be undisturbed and comfortable. The greatest gift you can give to yourself, your family and the Universe is to dissolve your negativities and find inner harmony. So give yourself this time.

You may like to record this visualisation on to a tape or ask a friend to read it to you.

Close your eyes and relax your body and mind. Breathe in and out of your chest, imagining it becoming warm and soft.

Remember a time when you felt bad about something. Replay this time in your imagination. Now bring in your negative mother. How does she look? What does she say or do to you? How do you feel after this negative input? Notice the sensations in your body.

Become aware of shining white steps appearing in your inner picture. They lead right up into the sky and out into the Universe. Far away in the distance you can see a glistening white mansion.

A Being of Light is coming into your scene and taking your negative mother up these steps. Your mother is knocking at the door of the mansion. When it opens, she is asking to be filled with love and for the wisdom to help you. She is invited inside.

Inside the white mansion she receives love and help and encouragement. You may go in with her or wait for her while she is healed.

She returns down the steps glowing, her consciousness expanded and her heart full of love. Now she offers you all the love, encouragement, support and wisdom you want and need. Relax with these good feelings for one minute.

Again, remember a time when you felt bad about something and picture the event in as much detail as possible. Now bring in your negative father. What does he

Everything can change

say or do to you? How do you feel after this negative input?

It is time for your negative inner father to receive healing at the great white mansion. Once more the Being of Light appears and takes him up the shining steps until he knocks on the door. When it opens, your father asks for the love and wisdom he needs to help you. He goes inside to receive whatever he needs, so that he can be truly open and loving with you. Go in with him or wait for him.

He is returning down the steps, shining with light, his consciousness expanded. He looks warm and full of love. Now he gives you the support, encouragement, love and wisdom you want.

Experience what this feels like. Notice how different your body feels. Breathing in comfortably, focus on the new sensations and relax for a minute.

Give your new inner mother a hug and say thank you. See the love in her eyes and take this love into the cells of your body.

Now give your new inner father a hug and say thank you. See the love in his eyes and take this love into the cells of your body.

Record what you experienced during your visualisation:

_____

_____

Getting our parents in perspective

We may feel enormous love, respect, caring and warmth towards our parents. And at the same time we may feel anger, frustration or resentment towards them. We may feel hurt, guilty, numb or confused when we think about them. Some people say they feel nothing for their parents or have no interest in them. This tends to mean that they have a tangle of unresolved emotions that they don't want to look at.

Our parents were once babies and small children. They had to survive in their surroundings with their parents. Generally speaking, by the time we become grandparents we have softened. We have dealt with a lot of life's problems and have become wiser and more mellow.

When our grandparents were parents to our parents as children, they were probably quite different. Almost certainly our parents had to deal with the same issues as us.

In order to understand how our parents became the people they did, treating us as they did, it is most helpful to talk to them about their childhood (as they perceived it). They may have had difficulties to contend with that we have no concept of. Understanding and awareness of another's hardships and feelings open us up to compassion and can dissolve some of our negative feelings.

If our parents are not available for us to talk to, the next best thing is to talk to other members of the family. Failing that, we need to sit down and spend a little time reflecting on what sort of childhood our parents had in order to become the adults they were. What were the circumstances of their childhoods? What might their parents have been like? What fears and beliefs did they bring into this life to deal with?

Being a parent is not easy. There is no way we can get it all right and there is no way our parents could get it all right for us. They did their best in the circumstances and with the mental and emotional equipment they had available to them at the time.

It helps to remember that we only ever talk to ourselves. So when we tell someone else off, we are talking to the aspect of that person that we perceive within us.

So if Dad was shouting at us for doing something wrong, he was really talking to the little boy inside himself that couldn't get it right. If

Mum told us we were unattractive, she was talking to the part of herself that believed she was unattractive. With this awareness we can start to give them back what belongs to them.

As we alter our attitude to our parents we send a different energy to them. We send them love instead of fear. It doesn't matter where they are. They may be alive. They may be in spirit. They may even have incarnated in another body. Wherever they are in the Universe, they will pick up our change in energy and it will heal something in them. It is never too late to heal our relationships.

1 *Write* what you know about your parents' childhood and/or imagine what sort of childhood they had to make them turn out as they did:

_____

_____

2 If they were small children now, what would they need from you?

_____

_____

3 Assume that they still need this. In what ways can you give them what they need?

_____

_____

You may like to record this visualisation on to a tape or ask a friend to read it to you.

Find a space where you can be quiet and undisturbed. Then close your eyes and relax.

Imagine your mother as a little girl of two or three. This little child desperately wants to be loved and cared for. See just how vulnerable and frightened she is inside. Small babies and children who are hurting and afraid may become angry or defiant or rude, so if she is difficult see how scared she is underneath.

As you recognise just how needy and afraid this little girl is, sit her on your knee and cuddle her until she feels safe enough to relax with you.

Talk to her very gently and lovingly. Ask her what she needs from you and listen carefully to her replies. Promise her that, now you understand, you will never hurt her feelings again and you will never let anyone else put her down or hurt her.

You may have to do this several times before she trusts you.

Now that she has relaxed and is receptive, remind her of all her good points until she glows with pleasure. Then put the little girl into your heart.

Now imagine your father as a small boy of two or three. Realise how vulnerable he is. What is he afraid of and how does he deal with his fear? He is only a small child who can't look after himself. He is defending himself or getting attention in the only way he knows how.

Be aware of just how afraid this little boy is. Sit him on your knee and cuddle him until he trusts you and relaxes. Then promise him that you will always try to understand him and will never hurt his feelings again.

Talk to him very gently and kindly. Ask him what he needs from you and listen to what he tells you. Give him

I'm lonely

I'm hurting

Your parents are
vulnerable too

the love and understanding he craves. Give him all the attention he needs.

Then tell him all the things you like about him and all his good qualities. Remind him of all the things he can do well.

Take your mother's little girl from your heart and take both children into a beautiful garden where the sun is shining and all the flowers are in bloom. Play with them. Experience having lots of fun with them and feel the barriers come tumbling down. Let yourself laugh and really enjoy this.

When you have done this look into their eyes and become aware of the love they hold for you. They may never have been able to connect with this love or express it in the outer world, so you may never have seen it before.

Let this love flow right into your heart and allow your heart centre to expand. Then let the love flow into every cell of your body and know that you are loved and lovable.

Feel this love flow as a beautiful pink light into your aura, filling it with this new energy. Let this new, soft, pink, loving energy flow out from you to other people in your life.

Record what you experienced during your visualisation:

_____

_____

Creating wise parents

Just imagine what your life would have been like if you had had a wise, loving, nurturing mother who always understood how you felt, who listened to you and believed in you. This wise mother always had encouraging words for you and reminded you of your positive qualities and successes. What is more she enjoyed being a woman and felt happy with her sexuality.

And imagine that your father was strong and supportive and fair. He too constantly encouraged you and helped you fulfil your potential. You totally trusted him to protect you, for he would never let anyone mess you around or take advantage of you. He enjoyed being a man and felt happy with his manhood.

If we had had parents like these our lives would have been different. However, none of us has these wise parents and as soon as we become conscious beings, our task is to provide this wise parenting for ourselves.

For most of us, a very big part of our consciousness is taken up with the voices of our negative parents. These are the voices in our heads that are constantly criticising us, warning us to be careful, reminding us of our failures or shouting at us for not being good enough.

And they only leave a small amount of room for a wise parent in our heads.

The minute we decide to listen as much as possible to the wise, strong, encouraging inner voice, and to ignore the negative voice, we are increasing the wisdom we have available to us.

We can literally say, 'Go away negative parents. What would my wise parents say?' and then listen to the positive wise advice.

When people do this, they are often surprised at the strength of the suggestions that come from their wise inner parents. And of course they realise that they are giving themselves help and advice and encouragement. It comes from within, not from outside.

I had the fascinating experience of having a medium describe to me an incredibly wise and powerful man, whom she felt was an archetypal father, standing by me. She could hear what he said and feel his presence. Then she suddenly realised that this was my very own wise father, whom I had created with my thoughts and who was there on the astral plane to

give me constant support and inspiration. 'You have created for yourself the father you always wanted,' she said to me.

We all need wise parents. It is immensely important and powerful and we can all do it for ourselves.

1 *Write down* all the good qualities your parents possessed and all the positive things they did for you.

When you have done this, remember that anything we perceive in another is within us, even if we are not yet in touch with that quality. Constantly read this list and focus on it.

_____

_____

2 If you had truly wise parents, what would they say to you now about your current problems and challenges?

_____

_____

3 What steps can you take to parent yourself wisely now?

_____

_____

Visualisation to create wise parents

Find a space where you can be quiet and undisturbed. If you can, raise the vibrations of this place with beautiful music, spiritual books, a candle, incense or flowers.

You may like to record this visualisation on to a tape or ask a friend to read it to you.

Close your eyes and relax your body. Take your time to breathe slowly and deeply and feel the tension draining away.

Imagine you have a wise, caring, loving and nurturing mother who encourages you. What does she suggest you do to look after yourself? She is reminding you now of your positive qualities and gifts. What does she mention? She loves you whatever you do or don't do. What does she say to encourage you?

She is very comfortable about being a woman and is helping you to be comfortable as a woman, or if you are a man she is helping you to feel at ease and comfortable as a man. Take time to listen to her reminding you that you are OK as a woman (or man). Experience how this feels. How different does your life become with this good feeling about your womanhood (manhood) and sexuality? How differently do you behave with the opposite sex? How differently do you behave with your own sex?

And now imagine that you have a wise, strong, supportive father who sees your potential and helps you reach it. He is encouraging and helping you.

He is very fair and firm so you feel totally safe to expand your comfort zones and try new things. No one can treat you badly or indifferently with this father around. He is so strong that your self-image and courage are bolstered. Experience how this feels. How different does your life become?

He is comfortable about being a man and is reminding you that you are totally acceptable as a woman (or man).

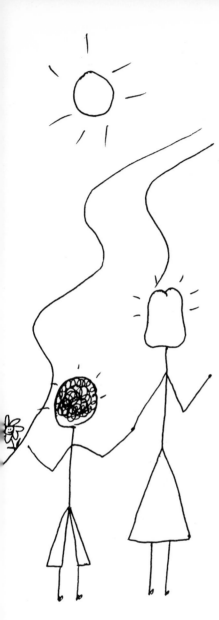

A sunny path, with
a wise parent

He makes you feel good. He helps you feel comfortable with your sexuality. Experience how this feels and imagine your relationships now that you are comfortable about your gender and your sexuality.

Now go back into your childhood. Imagine you are a toddler and visualise these wise parents guiding, loving and encouraging you.

Let these wise parents guide you from the age of three to the age of eight. Visualise this part of your childhood with your wise parents guiding you. Take time to experience this and heal this part of your life.

Now move to the ages of eight to thirteen and allow these wise people to parent you.

Now go through your teens with these wise, firm, supportive, caring parents and experience your teens in a new way.

Move through any difficult parts of your life and let your new wise parents help you. Allow your wise mother and father to advise, encourage and help you now. Listen to them. Feel inspired and strengthened and make the changes you need to make.

Open your eyes, feeling much stronger and more confident.

Record what you experienced during your visualisation:

_____

_____

The martyr

Most of us have a bit of the martyr in us! And if one of our parents was a martyr, then we will definitely be one, for martyrs beget martyrs.

Most carers and nurturers have quite a bit of the martyr lurking inside, because we deny our needs. Somehow, to admit our neediness will take away from the selflessness of our offering.

Whenever we say we're fine, when really we feel less than happy, we are being a martyr. For most of us it is so conditioned that we hardly realise we're telling lies. When we sigh as we get on with the washing-up, or solving someone else's problem, we're being a martyr.

When we feel misunderstood and unappreciated and that no one really realises how much work we do, we need to look at our inner martyr. Similarly when we feel that everyone expects us to deal with the problems and it really is too much, our martyr is at work. Some martyrs carry the can for other people's mistakes. Others feel they get the blame when it isn't their fault.

What our martyr does is suffer. Sometimes we suffer with loud sighs and eyes raised to heaven. Other times we suffer and seethe. Either way we hold masses of anger because we are not enjoying life. Of course we don't allow ourselves to go out and have fun because then we wouldn't be martyrs any more. So we can't accept help and we have to be seen to suffer. That is part of the game.

The aim of a martyr is to make other people feel guilty. 'I'll go out and earn money while you merely keep house.' 'I'll cook while you watch your programme on television.' It is very common for mothers to clean and cook and darn and sew while the rest of the family is having fun.

I never even realised I had a martyr streak until I did something with a sigh and my daughter immediately said, 'Mum, you martyr!' I suddenly realised how much of a martyr I was being. We had a good laugh, shared out the jobs and all went out to enjoy ourselves. From that moment I realised how often I had done this in the past and have since kept a close eye on my tendency to martyrdom.

When we play the martyr we are angry and we want to punish others. While we are trying to punish someone else, we are also turning it inward and punishing ourselves. As we realise this, it is appropriate to look at why we are angry and with whom. Anger is powerlessness and it is important to deal with the situation. Remember that the whole family of a martyr suffers, just as everyone who works for a martyr suffers.

Being a martyr may make us feel special or noble or saintly. Perhaps self-sacrifice is the only way we can get this good feeling. We may be a martyr because we feel terribly guilty about something. Perhaps we believe we are bad, so we have to suffer, and we punish everyone else at the same time. Decide to give it up today.

1 Checklist for martyrdom:
   a Was one of your parents a martyr?
   b Are any of your friends matyrs? They are mirrors.
   c Do you ever feel misunderstood or unappreciated?
   d Do you feel burdened but that you've got to do it?
   e Do you work hard and refuse help? Do you think others can't do the job as well as you can?
   f Do you feel you do everything and somehow get the blame?
   g Do you feel it is a hard life – and pretend you are coping?
   h Do you do things with a sigh?
   Record situations where you have a martyr tendency:

   _____

2 Remember a time when you were playing martyr. Who did you want acknowledgement from? Who did you want help from? Who were you angry with or trying to punish? What did you feel guilty about?

   _____

Visualisation to release your martyr

Find a space where you can be quiet and undisturbed. This is your time to heal yourself and you deserve it.

You may like to record this visualisation on to a tape or ask a friend to read it to you.

Before you start, go through the joints of your body, moving each one gently in circles and then stretching them. Do your toes, ankles, knees, hips, shoulders, neck, elbows, wrists and fingers. This starts the energy flowing in your body and will help you to relax.

Close your eyes and make sure your feet are solidly on the ground and that your spine is straight.

Visualise the people you feel angry with when you do all the work or when you are taking all the responsibility or carrying the blame. Line them up in front of you. What do you really want to say to them? Allow yourself to express your resentment and anger. What do you want to do to them? Do it. If you want to punish them, do it and get it out of your system.

Now look into their eyes and see their fear. They have felt your anger all this time. Peel away the surface fears until you are sure you have reached their core fear. What do they need from you? Open your heart and give them all that they need.

Recognise that their fear is a mirror of yours. What have you really wanted from them all this time? Let them give you the attention, validation, love, praise or thanks that you need. Open yourself up and allow yourself to receive what you truly want.

Now you find yourself walking up a hill carrying a great rucksack on your back. This is the burden you have been bearing. Take all the junk out of it and see what a load of rubbish you have been carrying. Dig a hole and bury all this rubbish piece by piece. Cover it over and be

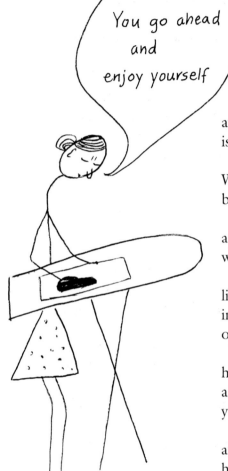

aware that it is being absorbed by the earth energy which is transmuting it all.

Plant in the soil seeds of joy and love and freedom. Water the seeds and bless them. Watch them grow into beautiful flowers.

Feel the sense of freedom. You are now more confident and much happier. Dance, sing, run or do anything you want in order to express the new you.

Imagine yourself asking clearly for the help you would like to have and receiving it graciously. See yourself working in a team with the others around you instead of on your own.

See yourself receiving acknowledgement. Let yourself hear all the compliments and nice things people are saying about the new you. Notice how these people now respect you.

Forgive yourself for the hard time you've given yourself and others. Visualise yourself joining in everything and having fun.

Open your eyes and return to the room and take decisions to laugh and enjoy life.

Write or draw what you experienced during your visualisation:

_____

_____

Choosing responses

When someone presses our buttons, which are our negative beliefs about ourselves, we feel old hurt feelings and react like a child. Moment by moment we are writing and acting out the play of our lives. Most of us react automatically when certain buttons are pressed. When we realise this we can make a choice to respond differently, and the entire script of our life changes.

A button is a belief we hold, such as 'I'm not valued, appreciated, understood, cared for,' or 'I feel rejected or unloved.' If, for example, someone's button is, 'I'm not valued,' he may work very hard to gain a sense of worth. He sits in the garden for two minutes and a friend comes by and says, 'It's all right for some who can lounge about.' Suddenly he feels no one values the work he does. He reacts with anger or coldness or self-justification and he feels bad.

He could choose to smile and say, 'Yes, I'm really enjoying the garden.'

Here is another example of button-pressing and how to deal with it. A mother came to see me because of increasing rows with her daughter. The mother was a nurturer. The daughter refused to eat breakfast. After years of struggle the mother accepted this. That Sunday she had taken her husband breakfast in bed and had hers in the kitchen. In walked her daughter and said, 'You've had scrambled egg for breakfast. You know I love scrambled egg and you didn't make me any.'

'I felt this terrible flash of rage,' the mother said. 'And I shouted at her. I felt she never appreciated me. We had an awful row.' She recognised that her daughter was making a statement about wanting to be loved, but her buttons overrode her caring, nurturing nature.

I asked the mother to close her eyes and see the daughter come into the kitchen that morning. She re-enacted the scene and felt the familiar tension in her solar plexus. 'How old does your daughter feel as she says this?' I asked.

'About four!' she replied.

'And how old do you feel?'

'Two! I often felt like this as a child. No one appreciated me, however hard I tried. No wonder we squabbled. She's four and I'm two.'

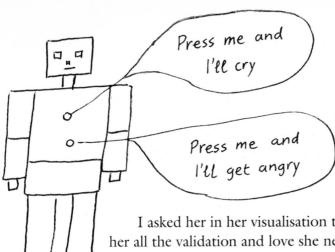

I asked her in her visualisation to pick up her two-year-old and give her all the validation and love she needed. When she had held and valued her child, she put the happy child into her heart. Then she felt open and loving enough to see her daughter's need. Her adult self smiled when she heard her daughter say, 'You didn't make me any scrambled egg.' She held out her arms and let her daughter run into them. She felt warm and loving.

She recognised that she would probably have to practise this again and again, but that if she gave herself a moment to think, no one could press that button again.

1 *Make a list* of all the things that press your buttons. Add to this list as you become more aware.

_____

2 Close your eyes and sense how old you become when these buttons are pressed. What does this child part of you need to receive or hear? Let your adult self give your child what it needs.
   Record what you experience:

_____

3 Close your eyes and sense what the person who pressed your buttons needs. We always attract our own fear so they will have the same fear as we do, however improbable this appears on the surface! Give them the love and reassurance you have given yourself.
   Record how this feels:

_____

Other people's buttons

If people often press our buttons we can be sure we are pressing other people's. If we are deliberately pressing other's buttons – in other words we know that certain things upset or anger them and we continue with our behaviour – then we must look at our motives. What are the payoffs for us?

Is being in trouble or disliked a familiar situation for us?

Does it push people away when they get too close?

Is it our only way of expressing our anger with them?

Is it an excuse to blame them for something?

Does it give us a feeling of power?

Is it our only way of getting attention?

Our behaviour is not helpful in developing us as whole people, so it is time to find appropriate ways to get what we need.

If we are pressing other people's buttons unconsciously – in other words we upset or anger people and we don't know how we are doing it – then it is helpful to put ourselves in the other person's place and sense what they are feeling. If we can talk to them about their lives and really listen and try to understand them, we can enter their world and give them what they really want from us.

Then we can choose to use the positive power of encouragement and praise instead of the negative power of button-pressing.

People usually need from us exactly the same as we want from them. I had a problem with my mother who constantly denigrated my work. She thought everything I did was ridiculous. That pressed a whole cluster of buttons for me and I felt frustrated and angry. I realise in hindsight that my angry hurt child deliberately set about pressing a few of her buttons in exchange.

One day I sat down to work out what I wanted from her. Of course, I wanted her to validate my work, to tell me she thought it was valuable and worthwhile.

I decided to talk to her about it. As I started, she suddenly burst out that she had loved being a nurse. It was her whole life and no one would

ever allow her to talk about it. The family told her to shut up or were bored and uninterested, so she closed down and never discussed it.

Instantly all was clear. There was no way she could validate my work until she felt that I had validated hers. She had given up nursing before I was born – over fifty years ago. And it still rankled inside her that her nursing skills weren't validated.

I could easily remember how caring my mother always was when we were ill as children. So it was easy for me to imagine her as an excellent, empathetic nurse. Now I could genuinely validate her work. The effect was instantaneous. She immediately started to ask questions about my work. Her attitude was transformed. I took care to encourage her instead of pressing her buttons. *And I felt better.*

1 Whose buttons do you press? What is the button and what is your payoff?

Name	*Button*	*Payoff*

2 What do you need from these people? For instance, perhaps you need to be loved, admired, respected, validated, listened to, understood . . .

_____

_____

3 What do they need from you? How can you meet their needs?

_____

_____

Visualisation to claim your power

Find a time and space where you can relax and be undisturbed. Remind yourself that it is your right to be powerful, so it is important for you to create this half hour or, if possible, a whole hour, for yourself!

You may like to record this visualisation on to a tape or ask a friend to read it to you.

Settle in a chair with your spine straight but relaxed. Let your eyelids gently close. Take a few moments to feel your feet heavy on the floor. Feel the heaviness float up your legs. Breathe down out of your legs to encourage this feeling. Then continue to do this through your body until you have a heavy and comfortable sensation.

Imagine yourself in a beautiful, flower-filled, summer garden. Take time to experience the green of the lawn and the colours of the flowers. Feel the warmth of the sun. Smell the fragrance of the day. Listen to the sounds of summer.

Someone who you upset or annoy is walking into your garden. You may press his or her buttons intentionally, or you may be unaware of what you are doing.

This other person is incredibly important to you as he can teach you a lot about yourself. You are intensely interested in finding out about him. Allow him to talk about himself and really listen. What does he say about his life and his feelings? If you can't get him to talk, just imagine what he would say.

Now imagine you have become that other person. How does it feel to be in his body? As that other person, talk about your childhood, your fears and your feelings. Speak about this person who annoys or upsets you? What do you feel about them? What do you want from them?

Come back into your own body and be yourself again. Now that you understand the person you have been

Wish your rival success

annoying or upsetting for so long, how do you feel about him?

Visualise yourself giving him what he needs. If he is a rival, know there is enough for everyone in a perfect way.

And now it is your turn to receive. What do you need from this person? Open yourself up to allow him to give you everything you want. Clearly visualise it and feel yourself getting it.

Take time to relax and enjoy the feelings.

Now that you feel empowered and loving, how differently can you relate to this person? What do you do or say differently? Give this person a hug and say what you really want to say to him. Then watch him walk out of the garden.

Take this good feeling into the outside world and sense yourself relating more happily to everyone.

Open your eyes.

Record what you experienced during your visualisation:

_____

_____

Relationships

There are two reasons for relationships on the Earth plane: one is growth and the other is so that we can have pleasure and fun.

Not a single person is in our lives by chance. We are like magnets. We send out magnetic energy and draw people to us according to this energy. So if we send out negative energy we will surely draw in negative people. If we send out beautiful positive energy we will magnetise beautiful positive people towards us.

All the people we have attracted into our lives are there as an exact reflection of the energy we hold, so if we pretend to be tremendously happy and bright to cover up a tendency to depression, we'll draw in a proportion of depressed people. If we are pleasers, covering up underlying resentment, we will attract resentful people.

The people and situations in our lives are a mirror for us to look into so that we can see what is really going on within us.

So everyone around us represents part of us in another body! If we stand in a room surrounded by mirrors, whichever way we turn we see a different aspect of ourselves. In the same way, the people in our lives reflect different aspects of our personality. We have relationships with them in order to learn about ourselves. Our learning is to accept the aspects they represent so that we can grow.

So if we don't get on with someone, there is only one reason. That person reminds us of an aspect of ourselves that we don't like. We may say, 'He makes me feel bad.' In fact he is mirroring a part of us that believes we are bad. Or we say, 'She makes me feel guilty.' As we know, no one can make us feel anything. So this person is reminding us of our own guilty feelings.

When we like someone it is because they make us feel good (warm, excited, happy, etc). They are reminding us of aspects of ourselves we feel comfortable about. They press a good button and we like them.

Even strangers arouse feelings in us because we project our own personalities on to them.

The more whole we are, and the more parts of ourselves we accept, the more people we get on with. All our relationships depend on how we feel about ourselves... not on the other person at all.

hall of mirrors

So there is only one important relationship – our relationship with ourselves. All the relationships we have directly mirror back to us our relationship with ourselves. And it isn't what those people are like that is the reflection – it is how we feel.

So one man may be a thief and a crook, while we are reasonably honest. If his thieving and dishonesty don't particularly bother us (we are non-judgemental and accepting), that is not the mirror. Then we have to look at how he makes us feel. Perhaps we feel vulnerable with him. Then he is a mirror for our vulnerability.

1   Write a list of the people you like. Which of your good qualities do they remind you of? What are their positive qualities?

Name	They remind me I am	Their good qualities

2   Write a list of the people you dislike. Which of your negative qualities do they remind me of? What do you dislike about them?

Name	They remind me I am	Their negative qualities

3a We all have polarities, so don't be surprised if opposites appear on your list: e.g. good quality – kind; negative quality – unkind. Write a list of your good qualities again. This reaffirms them.

b Look at your list of negative qualities. Now write a list of the opposite qualities and affirm these: e.g. miserable . . . write – contented. Affirmation – I am contented.

_____   _____

Visualisation to accept your positive self

Find a space where you can be quiet and undisturbed for as long as you need. Give yourself permission to create time to allow this healing to take place. It is important for you.

You may like to record this visualisation on to a tape or ask a friend to read it to you.

Close your eyes and allow yourself to relax. One by one put the worries and cares of the outside world into a box. When you have placed each one in the box, firmly shut the lid.

See in front of you all the people who make you feel good. Look at them one by one – all those kind, nice, generous, caring, beautiful, honest, fun-loving, successful, positive people who are in your life. As you look at each of these people, acknowledge their qualities. You would only notice these good qualities if they were within you. Recognise that all these people are mirroring back your positive qualities to you.

Repeat these good qualities to yourself as you see these people. As you accept and name your positive qualities, you are putting them one by one into your heart. You are an amazing person! Allow yourself to feel warm and loving and open-hearted.

Relax more deeply and breathe in golden light until your consciousness feels golden and accepting.

The greatest gift we can give another is to mirror their good qualities back to them.

Bring in one by one the people who reflect your negative qualities. Look into their eyes and recognise the fears which cause them to be negative. Feel the golden compassion flow from your heart centre to embrace them. Watch this golden energy dissolve their fear.

Now see your inner child who protected himself with these characteristics in order to survive. Acknowledge his fear. Remind him that he was very vulnerable then and did not know any other way of being. Remind him that you still love him and that he has all these positive qualities which you are going to help him express. Then embrace and love and accept your child.

When he feels totally safe and positively glowing put him in your heart.

Feel yourself becoming warm and golden. This wonderful golden energy is extending beyond your physical body and dissolving all darkness. Imagine this golden energy going round your home so that your home is in a beautiful glow. There are people and places trapped in the darkness of fear and hurt. So let this special light flow to any person or any part of the world where it is needed.

Record what you experienced during your visualisation:

_____

_____

Mirrors

When we really understand how the principle of mirrors works in the Universe we have an amazing tool for growth because everyone who comes into our lives gives us an opportunity to learn.

Here is an example of how life's mirrors work. If we hold a belief that we are stupid, we will attract people or situations which make us feel stupid. They reflect our feeling of stupidity back to us so that we see our belief in the mirror.

One woman I know actually wrote to tell me that her husband was an incredibly irritable, bad-tempered, angry man and she couldn't understand it because she was a mild, easy-going, nice person! When I met her, her jaw was rigid with tension. She was tremendously controlled, with a smile plastered on her face. Her husband was mirroring back to her all her suppressed anger.

A male client told me he was very successful but his closest friends were unsuccessful businessmen. My client was successful but was striving desperately against his fear of failure. His friends mirrored his fear of failure back to him.

So, instead of saying we don't like these people and trying to avoid them, our task is to change our belief. When we do change our belief, the reflection changes. Either the person moves away or our attitude is so different that we no longer feel the same way towards them. Usually we think they have changed!

Another way to look in the mirror is to say, 'What do I think of that person?'

If I disapprove of him, I have to look at where I disapprove of myself. He is, after all, me in another body. For example, if I dislike the way he plays out his sexuality, I have to look at my sexuality.

So we can look round at every single person in our lives – friends, relatives, colleagues, acquaintances – and see what qualities they reflect to us.

It is vital that we look at all the positive mirrors around us. In personal growth it is so easy to look at the negative stuff, in the belief that we are cleaning the mud out of the pond. However, we must keep shining the positive light of encouragement on to ourselves.

See your good points too.

So when we look at the people in our lives, we need to look at all their wonderful qualities. These are all mirrors reflecting aspects of ourselves back to us too.

Remember, the greatest gift we can give anyone is to mirror love back to them.

1 *List* the ten people closest to you. What do they mirror back to you, both positive and negative?

e.g. *Aunt Emmeline* She's a critical old witch.

Uncle Ethelbert He's thoughtful and friendly.

2 Close your eyes. Find these negative and positive parts within you and converse with them. For instance, take Aunt Emmeline and find the critical old witch aspect of yourself. Find out what made you become a critical old witch and start giving yourself what you need so you don't need to be like that any more.

Then take Uncle Ethelbert and talk to the thoughtful and friendly part of yourself and thank that part of you for being so helpful in your life.

Record what you learn:

Our shadow

As we have seen, everyone in our lives is there as a reflection of part of us. If we dislike them, they are mirroring to us an aspect of ourselves that we dislike. If we really hate them, then they are a real gift in our lives for they are showing us our shadow.

Our shadow is the unacceptable aspect of ourselves that we deny. We usually use a lot of energy to keep our shadow aspects hidden from our awareness. We know what our suppressed aspects are because they are the things we hate in others.

Take a nice, unassertive man. He tries to please people and feels very powerless. And because he gives away his power, he will be suppressing a good deal of anger. Inevitably he will attract the reflection of what he is burying . . . powerful angry people. Not surprisingly he hates these people because he can't handle his own power or anger, so he can't cope with theirs.

The more out of balance we are, the deeper the shadow. So a really over-the-top pleaser will have a very deeply suppressed shadow of anger.

People who persecute gays, for example, haven't come to terms with their own sexuality, so they try to stamp out their shadow when they see it in others.

Our shadow can be anything from deep black to grey. The more we want to be thought of as nice, the more we bury, hide and deny the opposite, our nasty self, and the blacker it is. So the angry, resentful or mean feelings are like a volcano inside us. Suddenly, these repressed feelings pop out because it takes a lot of psychic energy to keep suppressed feelings down.

If the gentle person becomes violent under the influence of alcohol, his shadow is emerging. Under stress the rigidly honest, upright person might shoplift. The puritan who preaches against sex might have a fling.

The compulsive nurturer's shadow is needy. The over-carer's is callous. The over-generous person's is a mean streak. When any part of us is out of balance we have a shadow. It appears as characters in dreams. Over-the-top responses indicate a lurking shadow and so do the people and things we hate in our lives.

Whenever we feel judgemental about anyone it shows us something

we suppress in ourselves. When we acknowledge our fallibility and accept it in ourselves, the other person no longer bothers us.

And when we integrate the nice with the nasty we can be genuine, feel good about ourselves and be clear in our dealings with others.

We can't stamp out our shadow. We must light it up with acceptance and non-judgement. Then we can be in balance, just like the sun at the point of equilibrium above us. There it casts no shadow.

1 *Identifying the shadow*

Who do you hate or really dislike? What qualities do you really hate in them? These are your shadow aspects. The more deeply denied they are, the more likely you are to tear this page out or to say this exercise is stupid. Stay with it. It is important.

e.g. I hate Zoe. She's sexually free, slovenly and unprofessional. In this case I will most likely be sexually somewhat inhibited, smart and extremely professional. I cannot let my sexuality and my career flow because I am using so much energy to hold my shadow down. It is time to release it.

People I hate   *What I hate about them*

_____   _____

_____   _____

2 What changes are you ready to make?

_____

_____

Visualisation to understand your shadow

Make time and space for yourself where you can be quiet and undisturbed while you do this exercise.

You may like to record this visualisation on to a tape or ask a friend to read it to you.

Close your eyes and breathe in and out very gently and evenly. It is time to let go of the outside world. Bring the focus of your mind to your heart centre and be aware of the rise and fall of your chest.

When you feel comfortably warm and relaxed, imagine an orange, glowing sun rising in your chest. Allow it to open up your chest and radiate out around you.

Now focus on one of the characteristics or qualities that you hate about someone. Notice where your body becomes most uncomfortable.

Focus on this uncomfortable part of your body, breathing gently and comfortably into it, and allow an animal to emerge from there. Stay calm and relaxed. You are safe in your inner world and nothing can hurt you.

This animal is very afraid and may be very angry because you have been denying it for so long. Tell it quietly that you would now like to get to know it and understand it. Explain that you are not going to deny it or reject it any more, whatever it does.

The animal holds a lot of pent up emotion so allow it to roar, scream or make any noise it needs to or shake with fear. It has had to bury its feelings for so long because it thought you would hate it and abandon it if it let go. All the time listen intently to whatever it has to tell you, without judging or interrupting in any way.

When you have heard what it is saying, and feel you understand, ask what it needs from you. Take time and care about giving it what it needs. Become friends with it. Lovingly stroke or caress it.

Allow the animal to return into your body and notice if your physical sensation has changed.

Repeat this exercise with any other shadow qualities or characteristics you need to look at. Then open your eyes and know that you have unblocked your flow a little.

Record what you experienced during your visualisation:

_____

_____

Healing relationships

If our relationships aren't working the first thing to recognise is that we can't change the other person. They are only a reflection of an aspect of us. We have to change ourselves.

In order to heal our relationships we must stop expecting others to meet our needs. We are responsible for our own happiness, our own independence, our own security. When we make someone else responsible for aspects of our lives, we have a leaning relationship. They become our prop and when the prop moves, we collapse. So the relationship is stuck together by fear of not being able to manage alone.

First we must take stock of the things we need to make us whole. Then we can start to provide these things for ourselves. If we need emotional support perhaps we can join a support group. If we need more happiness it is time to do what gives us joy. When two people are whole, they stay together because they enjoy being together.

When we focus on the positive in someone else, those qualities grow. When we are in love we only see that person's good qualities and when we hate them we only focus on the qualities we dislike in them. Some people swing from one out-of-balance state to the other. That is not love. Love means accepting people as they are.

Be aware that the person we are relating to is picking up our thoughts. They hear what we say and, at another more subtle level, they pick up our thoughts and respond to them.

If our child says, 'I feel sick when I go to Auntie's,' he is trying to tell us something. He may be saying he feels abandoned by us. He may want to tell us he is being bullied, or the gas is leaking or he is being sexually assaulted by someone there. If we carelessly respond with, 'Don't be silly. Of course you don't feel sick,' we will never know.

If our partner says, 'You never have time for me these days,' he is trying to communicate something. If we respond with, 'Don't be silly, we're always doing things together,' he doesn't feel validated. We don't get to understand him and a wall grows between us.

The greatest healings take place when we listen to the other person. By that I mean, when we sit and hear what they say to us, without interruption, without judgement, really trying to understand their reality.

What is it that we want from them? Is it validation, acceptance, trust, consistency? That is almost certainly what they want from us too. When we start giving it to them, we will build better relationships.

1 In what way are you needy and dependent on your parents, partner, children or other relationships? Be very honest.

_____

_____

2 What do you need to do to make yourself whole in these areas?

_____

_____

3 What programme of self-nurturing and expansion do you propose to start for yourself? e.g. 'I am starting a class in astrology.' 'I am booking a massage.'

_____

_____

4 Listen to someone today with your full attention and *record* what you learn:

_____

_____

It's time to get down the walls.

Go to a place where you can be quiet and undisturbed. You may like to record this visualisation on to a tape or ask a friend to read it to you.

Make yourself comfortable, sitting in a chair with your spine straight.

Close your eyes and put your feet firmly on the ground. Let them become heavy and relaxed and sense yourself being earthed.

Put your hand over your heart centre and allow the tension to flow out of your body.

Imagine a golden ball of light in the Universe above you. This ball is pure love and wisdom. It is beginning to move slowly down towards you until it rests gently on your crown centre. Feel your scalp relaxing.

Now it is moving down into your mind, soothing your mind and filling your consciousness with love. Breathe in and out of your mind.

Then feel it floating down until it rests under the palm of your hand. Sense its warmth. Let it move into the centre of your chest, right into your heart centre. Feel it expanding and filling your chest with love.

In front of you see yourself and the person with whom you want to heal your relationship.

How big is the wall between you?

What colour is it?

Dissolve the wall with golden love from your heart centre.

If you sat and listened to what this person opposite you really wanted to say to you, what would he say? Truly listen now and hear.

Understand this person's fear that has made him treat you as he has done. Recognise that he is mirroring your own fear. Forgive him. Then forgive yourself.

Now open your eyes and start thinking in a different, more loving way about this person.

Record what you experienced during your visualisation:

_____

_____

For a little girl, the first role model for her sex is her mother. If her mother feels comfortable as a woman, the little girl unconsciously picks this up and learns that it is safe to be a woman.

And the first role model of how the opposite sex feels about her is her father. So the way he relates to her is vital for how comfortable she will feel with men later in life.

And, of course, it is the same for a boy. His mother is his role model for his relationship with the opposite sex. If she loves his father and is comfortable with men and at the same time she loves her son, he can grow up to feel secure with women.

However, when a mother is angry with her father because he wasn't there for her, her daughter will almost certainly follow the pattern and attract a husband with whom she can be angry. If she is lonely, dissatisfied, bored and feels unattractive, she will develop a pattern of creating distant relationships with men she is angry with. And these men will treat her as unattractive.

The son of this angry mother feels that men are bad, so he must be bad. He can't please his mother because she is angry with men and he believes he can't make a woman happy. He's on a path to attracting and creating unsatisfactory relationships with women.

From our beliefs we create patterns, which are behaviours which we keep repeating. They are unconscious. Our patterns are magnets, attracting the perfect people to slot into our beliefs.

Here is an example. A man was continuously criticised by his father. His belief was: 'I must have been bad or he wouldn't have said those things. I deserve to be punished.' He attracted partners with a tendency to punish, and allowed them to abuse him. His pattern was to be put down and abused in his relationships.

The little boy whose mother had no time for him ends up believing that women have no time for him. His adult pattern is to attract women who aren't really interested in him. If a woman finds time for him he acts according to his pattern to distance them until they get interested in other things.

The girl whose Dad left when she was small has a belief that it is not

safe to love men: 'When I love someone, they leave me.' This becomes her pattern, as she in turn attracts in men with a pattern of leaving. Alternatively, she may attract a safe man and then cling on so tightly that she stifles him until he leaves. Then she can complain again: 'When I love someone, they leave me.'

1 What messages did you pick up as a child about how you deserved to be treated?

_____

_____

2 How do you behave which allows people to treat you like this?

_____

_____

3 What messages did you pick up as a child about how the opposite sex should be treated?

_____

_____

4 How do you behave towards the opposite sex?

_____

_____

Healing our patterns

Healing our patterns always involves healing our relationships with our inner parents. Until we have done this we will attract partners or people who have the same qualities as our parents had or who make us feel the same way.

One thing we can't do is resist our patterns. The more we resist something or someone, the more we focus on it. This means we are constantly putting the picture of what we resist into our unconscious mind. The work of our unconscious mind is to produce for us what we picture.

So, to heal our patterns, we need to picture what we want coming from other people. Then we have to imagine the feeling of getting what we want. That can be surprisingly difficult. If we have never let ourselves be nurtured, it can be overwhelming to let ourselves receive nurturing.

If we think one parent was wonderful and the other terrible, we will be setting up difficult patterns for ourselves. There is no such thing as one good and one bad parent. They colluded with each other to create this impression based on their patterns. We need to recognise how they both made this happen. As we accept and forgive both of them, we balance ourselves out and start to heal some of our patterns.

Having recognised our patterns, we need to make affirmations to change our beliefs. This will shift our surface beliefs and should start a cycle of deeper and deeper change.

If this doesn't go deep enough, we have to find the source of our problem. The source will usually be in another life, but it is often enough to heal something from our childhood. It is as if clearing a blockage from a gutter will allow sufficient flow for the rest of the pipe to clear itself. If it doesn't, we need to heal another life or lives. This can often create fundamental shifts, allowing us to feel so loved and lovable that our negative patterns dissolve.

Sometimes we need to acknowledge and express deeply trapped emotions in order to heal something. It helps to do this with the support of a therapist or in a workshop.

So if we have a pattern of failure, we need to focus on success. We make affirmations of success. We visualise success and we feel the imagined

feeling of success. We begin to act as if we are successful.

Then we do a visualisation to find our inner child who believed it was a failure and we creatively start the healing process. The next step is to do a visualisation to go back into one or more past lives to look at and creatively release the source of our belief.

Our essence is love. To find our essence is to heal our patterns.

1 What are your patterns? (For instance: 'Men never support me.' 'I leave first.' 'I always have a husband and a lover.' 'Women want my money.' 'Men only want my body.' 'No one understands me.' 'No one listens to me.')

_____

_____

2 What do you now wish to attract or create in their place?

_____

_____

3 *Write* the affirmations you are now going to use, up to a thousand times per day, in order to establish healthy patterns!

_____

_____

Visualisation to heal your patterns

Find a space where you can be quiet and at peace. Make sure you are undisturbed for the time you need to do this exercise.

You may like to record this visualisation on to a tape or ask a friend to read it to you.

Settle into a chair with your spine straight and your feet on the floor.

In your imagination walk into a beautiful meadow. Sense the soft green grass and feel your bare feet in the grass. Take time to be aware of all the sensations.

Listen to the sound of the birds, the tinkling of a stream and the faint rustle of leaves in the balmy breeze. Relax into your inner scene in your sunny meadow and become aware of the smell of the warm summer's day.

Think of unhelpful ways in which you behave or situations you keep finding yourself in and be aware of the feeling inside you. Where is the tension in your body? What does it feel like?

Take yourself back in time and imagine how big you were when you first had this sensation. How old do you feel inside? Where are you? What is happening around you?

Bring in your parents and in your imagination let them give you what you needed in order to be whole. If you cannot do this because your parents were absent or too damaged themselves, bring in your wise parents and let them heal your inner child.

Take time to imagine yourself behaving comfortably and appropriately, knowing that you are OK and you have a solid basis of support and love. Focus on the good feelings.

Past
° Life
Pattern

Child
° pattern

Adult
pattern

It's time to change

It is time now to clear your pattern at a deeper level. Imagine a golden light from your crown centre to your Higher Self and then from your Higher Self right up to the Source, the Godhead. Ask here to know what happened in a past life which caused you to form the belief which made you create this pattern.

Relax and allow pictures or thoughts or insights to come up for you. Be aware of how you felt in those circumstances so long ago. What thoughts and beliefs did you bring forward? If you did something you regret, it is time to forgive yourself for what happened then. Try to understand and forgive anyone who injured you. Fill your inner scene with golden light. Let the scene fade.

Fill yourself now with that lovely golden sensation. Creatively visualise yourself with a positive, loving, joyous pattern and enjoy the good feeling. Focus on the good things that you are now able to attract.

Take as long as you like to enjoy the scenes and sensations. Then, when you are ready, open your eyes.

Record what you experienced during your visualisation:

_____

_____

Uncording

Whenever we send a thought to something or someone we send an energy impulse to them. A casual thought will be dissolved but when we send a strong and consistent thought, it forms a binding cord which ties us to the other person. Through this cord energy flows. These cords can be seen in many forms, from steel rods to tangles of barbed wire to ropes. While they remain we are not free to be ourselves.

The most powerful attachments are to our parents. When these are not released at puberty in a natural way, we remain negatively corded to them and are not emotionally free to pursue new relationships.

Thoughts between couples are often quite thorny too and many couples have found their relationships improve dramatically when the negative cords are removed. Alternatively, they may find that they can easily separate or divorce when whatever has been entangling them is untied. It is not helpful for anyone's spiritual growth to be negatively corded to someone else.

These cords can be seen by clairvoyants but it is better when we visualise them ourselves. They may appear in almost any form.

Usually I ask the client to visualise himself sitting in a circle and invite the person he wishes to uncord from to sit in a circle in front of him. He visualises light going round the two circles in a figure of eight. This gives his unconscious mind the message: 'I wish to release from this person or thing.' It is helpful to do this exercise daily for a week or two before the uncording.

Energy flows through the cords into the other person's body. Our energy is our power, our life force, and we have allowed it to flow to someone else. Having the wrong energy in our body is like having the wrong blood in our body! It is time to claim our own energy back. This is done by visualising magnets pulling our energy back into our body and people can often feel this as a physical sensation.

Occasionally people feel a sense of loss after an uncording. This can be uncomfortable but also shows how necessary it was.

When we free ourselves from attachment to things and people, we are free to enjoy them without having to possess them. It is liberating.

I can't be happy unless I have . . . .

JOB

£

1 The place where the cords enter the body indicate emotional attachments as follows:

base centre I need you to help me survive.
sacral centre I want you emotionally or sexually.
solar plexus I need your energy.
heart I want you to love me.
throat I want to communicate (and daren't).
third eye I'm watching you psychically.
crown Follow my teachings. I own you.
hands I manipulate you.
feet I pull you off your feet, trip you up.

Sense where you are attached to different people and *record* what you sense:

_____

_____

2 *Make a list* of people you need to detach from:

_____

_____

3 *Make a list* of things you are attached to. (We know when we are attached to something because our happiness depends on having it.)

_____

_____

Find a quiet place and arrange to be left alone. You may like to record this visualisation on to a tape or ask a friend to read it to you.

Close your eyes and relax.

Visualise yourself sitting in a circle and see an empty circle in front of you. Invite the person you wish to uncord from to sit in the circle in front of you. You may prefer to trust your unconscious mind and just let whoever is right come in.

Explain to the person in the circle that you are now freeing both of you emotionally. Let light flow in a figure of eight round the two circles for a few moments.

Pick up a magnet which is energised for your energy only and hold it in front of your solar plexus towards the

other person. Feel your own energy being drawn back to you. When you have finished let him pick up a magnet which is energised for his energy and allow him to draw his energy out of you. Put the magnets out of the way behind you.

Visualise the cords between you. Imagine yourself reaching out your hands and running them along the cords. Feel their size and texture.

Cut them in the middle with golden spiritual scissors (or something bigger, like a saw, if necessary). Very gently pull the cords out of the other person's body and throw the cords on to a bonfire to burn.

Take time to clean and heal the wounds where the cords have been and then seal the wounds with a cross in a circle.

Thank the person you have uncorded from for teaching you whatever you needed to learn from them. Forgive them for being human and forgive yourself too.

It is time to let them go. Wave goodbye as they depart from your inner scene, leaving you emotionally free.

In your inner scene take off your clothes, which represent the old negative habits, and throw them on to the bonfire. Find some water to swim in and totally cleanse and purify yourself. Then come out into the sunshine and express your freedom by running or dancing or in any way you want.

You will find new clothes, representing the new you, laid out. Put them on and experience how they feel. Walk down your new pathway, free and happy.

Record what you experienced during your visualisation:

_____

_____

Guilt

Guilt is the most insidiously destructive of all emotions, because it implies internalised resentment and an avoidance of responsibility for this.

The controlling voice of our inner parent tells us what we should or ought to do. If we don't do these things, our pleaser will make us feel guilty. At the same time we resent doing what we feel obliged to do and then punish ourselves for feeling resentful. We place ourselves in a no win position.

When we feel guilty we attract a punishment. This may be in the form of accidents or illness or some other nasty event which will give us emotional or physical pain.

Guilt, like any fear, is dissolved by understanding, love and forgiveness.

Everything we do in our lives, good or bad, is done in an effort to learn that we are Beings of Love. Naturally we do some bad, hurtful things to ourselves and others in the process of learning.

It is no different from a child falling over while he is learning to walk. It isn't bad to fall over, it is part of a learning process. If the child kept remembering how awful it was to fall over – and reminding himself of the pain – he would never learn to walk. So he automatically focuses on his goal of being able to walk.

And we have a choice. We can say, 'I'm a bad bad person for doing that and I am never going to let myself forget in case I do it again. So I'll keep beating and punishing myself to remind myself how bad I am.' This is the child staying stuck where he has fallen over.

Or we can say, 'Yes, I did what I did then because that's what I was learning then. By doing that (even if I did it fifty times and still do it sometimes) I am learning that it doesn't feel good, so I'm modifying my behaviour or attitude. I forgive myself and continue towards my goal to be a Being of Light.' This is taking responsibility for our actions.

There is a false religious teaching that we are all sinners and must suffer. This is not a teaching of love. Love teaches joy and forgiveness and encourages us to move forward. The verb *sinnen* originally meant 'to aim at a target and miss'. Love teaches us to aim for the light and try, try, try again if we don't succeed.

Because we believe we are bad and guilty, we punish ourselves and make ourselves suffer for aiming at love and not quite making it.

Our Spiritual Self is a Being of Love. Our human self is still learning. Our aim is to integrate the two.

1 *Write a list* of things which make you feel guilty:
   e.g. 'I feel guilty about sex outside a relationship.'
   'I feel guilty because I stole a pencil ten years ago.'

   _____

   _____

2 Whose voice is telling you that you are bad? What are they telling you and what are they threatening you with?

   _____

   _____

3 Now *write your response* to your inner voice, expressing your resentment, claiming your freedom, forgiving yourself if necessary and claiming your power to do what you want:

   _____

   _____

Jealousy

Anyone who is jealous believes there is only a limited amount of love. In fact when we open our hearts there is enough love for everyone and the more we open our hearts the more love flows through.

However when we are jealous we fear that we aren't lovable enough or there isn't enough love for us or that somehow other people get more love than we do. We close our heart centre and make lack of love our personal reality.

When we close our heart centre with jealousy we need to work from inside, building up confidence, interests and self-esteem.

When we are jealous we fear abandonment. After all, if we feel unlovable why should anyone want to stay with us. And when we are afraid of being rejected or abandoned, we need to keep others emotionally or even financially dependent on us.

If we find we are trying to control others, mentally, financially or emotionally, it is time to let go. It is time to uncord all these people. When we truly love others we free them. Then they stay because they want to, not because they are afraid to leave. As we make more space in our hearts, more people and more love flow into our lives.

Sexual jealousy is saying that we are not confident in ourselves as a sexual being. In this case if our partner is unfaithful it will be an insult to our soul. Because we don't believe in our manhood or womanhood we will allow ourselves to be incredibly undermined. When we are totally confident in our masculinity or femininity we can allow others freedom, and they can choose to be faithful because they want to be. And if a partner is sexually unfaithful we know it is their problem and remain quite secure in our sexuality.

When we are possessive we hold on desperately for fear of losing love. Again our heart centre is closed because we believe that love is limited. This means we have to hang on to what we have got.

Greed too is based on a belief that there is not enough, so we had better grab what we can while we can. Usually we are substituting material possessions for love. Again we need to let go and open up to more of the Universal Energy flowing through us.

When we envy, we wish we had what someone else has, whether it is gifts, qualities, possessions or love. When we open ourselves up and say thank you for what we have, more and more flows through us. We become magnets for good things.

When we are in harmony with ourselves and with life we attract wonderful things into our lives. Good luck, good fortune and happy relationships are all automatically attracted to the harmonious energy we are sending out.

1 What or who are you jealous, envious or possessive of?

_____

_____

2 Work out what the underlying fear is in each case. Then make an affirmation to let it go.

Fear   *Affirmation*

_____   _____

_____   _____

3 Draw your heart and make it open and welcoming:

Visualisation to free yourself of guilt

Tell me about it

I'm bad

Find a place where you can be quiet and alone for as long as you need to.

You may like to record this visualisation on to a tape or ask a friend to read it to you.

To raise your vibrations and purify your space, light an incense stick.

Close your eyes and feel yourself relax as you breathe in the perfume. Take time to let your muscles unwind.

Think of something that makes you feel guilty. Focus on your solar plexus and breathe into it.

Allow an animal which represents guilt to jump out of your solar plexus. Look at the animal and notice how it is acting. It may be cowering away, or looking shifty or acting with bravado or in some other way. Simply observe. As you watch the animal, become aware of how it is feeling. Sense its fears and needs.

Be very understanding as you allow it to talk. Let it say anything it wants to say. It may have a lot of resentment, pain or bad feelings to express. It may be terrified.

When the animal has finished speaking, assure it that you don't judge it and that you will remain friends with it. Promise it that you will never punish it again.

Creatively visualise ways for the animal to start regaining its pride in itself.

Then the two of you can have fun together.

When you have finished let the animal return into your solar plexus, feeling much happier and more relaxed.

Open your eyes.

Record what you experienced during your visualisation:

_____

_____

Visualisation to release your jealousy

welcome!

Find a space where you can be comfortable, relaxed and undisturbed. Raise the vibrations in your space by making sure it is clean and tidy. If possible put in beautiful flowers, candles, spiritual books.

You may like to record this visualisation on to a tape or ask a friend to read it to you.

Whenever you are jealous of someone else you shut your heart and believe that in some important way they are better than you are. You also believe that you are therefore lesser and will be rejected.

It is time to change you, so that you know deep within that you are acceptable on every level. All beautiful qualities come from within and this process starts in the creative mind.

Shut your eyes now. What are you jealous of? Take a few moments to remember in what ways you imagine someone is better than you.

Now imagine you are perfect in those ways, e.g. you have a perfect body, beautiful face, wonderful sense of humour, charisma, any qualities you want. Start visualising happy scenarios with the new you in them. Really feel what this is like. Enjoy it all. Then take all the things you are envious of in others and imagine you have these things in equal measure.

Create imaginative scenarios of you with it *all* now. Enjoy it. Feel it. Really live it in your mind. Know you are starting to create what you want for yourself. See yourself getting all you want.

Feeling yourself as talented, lovable, beautiful and perfect in every way, see yourself spreading happiness and love with your new qualities.

Let the perfect you go into specific difficult relationships or situations in your life and experience them differently. Be very aware of how much people love the new you. See how they respond differently to this aspect of you.

Feel your heart opening and being filled with love. It is as if your heart is now wide open and welcoming and you love everyone.

Write or draw what you experienced during your visualisation:

_____

Anger

Our *kundalini* energy, the life force which gets things done, is clear bright red. This energy protects us. It gives us vitality. When this is flowing it is a powerful force, which gives us the ability to help people in need.

It is when our red anger energy is mixed with fear that it becomes a problem, for then we try to hide it. Fear is black. Suppression is brown. When the red is mixed with black or brown, our anger becomes stuck. It becomes a murky red and this dark blob within us attracts difficult people or situations into our lives.

It takes an enormous amount of energy to hold repressed anger down and this is a common cause of tiredness. When we hold down any emotion we always feel powerless to get the love and validation we want. It is only when we feel powerless that we use anger to get our own way: 'If you don't do this I'll be angry.'

When we use anger in this way it is also a cry for help. It is telling us that there is something wrong in our lives.

Here are the steps to deal with anger.

First we need to understand the fear which lies under our anger. For instance, our anger may stem from fear of rejection, fear of not being good enough or fear of not being understood.

Then we must stay calm. If we cry we give our power away. If we shout and get angry we also give it away. To deal honestly with the situation, we need to be in command.

We must be careful not to blame the person or situation. After all, we attracted it to learn from. The moment we blame someone else they will put up their defences and we won't get anywhere. If the other person becomes defensive it is because we have somehow blamed them. It may be with our thoughts. It may be in our voice, in our body language or in our unspoken attitude. If we have been hanging on to the anger for a long time, it is very easy to keep a bit of it and blame the other person.

We don't need to justify our feelings. Our feelings are just that – *our feelings*. Needing to justify ourselves gives our power away.

When we remain open, and explain that we want to heal ourselves, magic happens. After all, the other person is us in another body and their fear is a mirror of ours. If our hearts are partially closed we may have to

do this several times. But when we open our hearts, and explain how we feel, we reclaim our power, relationships heal, and our anger dissolves.

1 Who or what makes you angry?

_____

_____

Note: If we say we are angry for someone else, we are identifying with the victim. The victim is an aspect of ourselves which we have placed outside ourselves. Often it is a way of avoiding responsibility and the Universe draws it to our attention in this way. So we need to ask ourselves, 'What part of me does the victim relate to?'

2 Without blame or self-justification, with your heart open, *write a letter* to the person you are angry with, expressing how you feel. You do not need to post this letter.

_____

_____

3 Put a cushion on a chair in front of you and imagine it is the person you are angry with. Practise talking aloud to this person about your feelings, again without blame or self-justification, and with your heart open. How does it feel?

_____

_____

Hurt

Most of us have layers of hurt and anger. They are like layers of an onion. We peel away some hurt and find anger underneath. Then off comes the anger and more hurt comes up.

Hurt and anger are very similar. Like anger, hurt is emotional blackmail. It too is used as a manipulation to get someone to do something. The victim's cry, 'You hurt me,' is a wonderful form of punishment calculated to make someone feel guilty so that they toe the line.

Hurt is a refusal to forgive. As long as we refuse to forgive, we are keeping old emotional wounds open.

It is a choice like any other emotion. Just like guilt and anger, we feel that by hanging on to hurt, we will prevent it from recurring. However when we hang on to hurt we live it constantly. We never allow ourselves to pass through it to the next stage.

Where we find we are holding on to hurt we need to feel, acknowledge and express the original pain. So we have to let go of our avoidance tactics and relive the hurt for only a moment, to free ourselves.

When we forgive the other person and ourselves, we remove the block from our heart centre–and also the block that has probably crystallized in our physical bodies.

We are all responsible for our own feelings of hurt. We are not responsible for anyone else's feelings. They have to deal with their own.

It is not our task to pussyfoot around people protecting their feelings.

However we have a responsibility to every human, animal, plant or mineral on the Earth plane. This means that we don't go round deliberately hurting others.

When we are totally open and honest about our feelings then other people pick up our clarity and feel safe. We hurt others when we are unclear. Then we are ambivalent, confused and possibly dishonest about what we feel. That really does manipulate people emotionally and causes a lot of pain.

So our task is to open our hearts and forgive those who have hurt us. Then we reap enormous rewards, as love comes flowing into us from all directions. All friendships and relationships are enriched, as we take the walls away from around our hearts.

At the same time, with our hearts open, we need to learn to be clear and honest about our feelings towards others. Then our throat centre opens. We stop pleasing, being a martyr, hanging on to guilt, anger and resentment, and start living.

1 Who or what do you feel hurt by?

2 How did you cause them to treat you like this?

3 I am now willing to forgive the following:

4 I also totally forgive myself for:

Visualisation to deal with anger

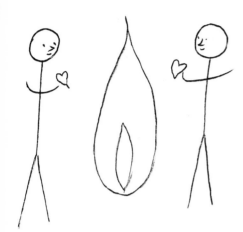

There is no
separation.
We are one.

Claim your power by making time and space for yourself to do this exercise. Make sure you are undisturbed and the phone is off the hook.

You may like to record this visualisation on to a tape or ask a friend to read it to you.

Sit quietly with your eyes closed. You may like to stroke your hands down over your aura a few inches from your body. If you sense warm and cool patches, just even them out gently as if you are stroking a cat.

Breathe comfortably and relax down into your inner space. Reach out your cupped hand and very gently catch a small spark of Universal Love. Carefully and protectively place this spark in your heart centre. Keep your cupped palm over your heart centre and feel the spark growing until it is a Flame of Love. Feel yourself connected to the Universal Flame.

See the person you feel angry with. Understand your anger by allowing the fear to surface. You may see yourself as a frightened child or see a situation in another life. Go lovingly into your inner picture and heal whatever you see. The Flame of Love in your heart will help you. When you have satisfied your inner need, become aware of the wall your anger has created between you and the other person. Look into their eyes. See their fear, which is a mirror of yours, and which is causing them to behave in this way.

As you recognise it, pour the Flame of Love on to the wall and dissolve it.

Now sit with them and explain how you feel and tell them you wish to heal your anger and the relationship. Listen to their feelings too.

As you feel your anger slip away, embrace and thank your new friend.

You are now feeling nurtured and much more powerful. What benefits will this new feeling bring in your life?

Visualise the empowered you living your life more effectively.

Record what you experienced during your visualisation:

Visualisation to let go of hurt

That's five lives of the same hurt

Go to a quiet space where you can feel relaxed and where you will not be disturbed. You may like to record this visualisation on to a tape or ask a friend to read it to you.

Close your eyes and breathe deeply. You are in a beautiful meadow and about to start a journey up a mountain. Take your time to walk to the mountain and start up the pathway. Notice if it is easy or difficult, straight or winding. When you are halfway up the mountain, the path winds through a green glade and you may rest here.

Higher up is a clear blue lake where can pause to paddle or swim. Near the top there is a waterfall. Relax and watch it cascading.

Now stand at the summit of the mountain. You are floating out of your body. You are above the planet looking down at it. Be aware of its size and colour. Look around you at the vast Universe. Notice the wonderful colours and all the love energy that is out there.

As you look down on to Planet Earth, sense all the lives you have had. In that context how important do these hurts seem?

Look down again and see all the people who have hurt you. Be aware of how the earthly you put up walls to stop those people from getting close. That is why they hurt you.

From this higher perspective see the hurts which caused them to behave as they did.

Open your arms and your heart. Sense yourself radiating golden energy. One by one let each of these people enter your heart and merge with you.

Breathe in deeply a golden colour for a few minutes.

Then feel yourself moving down until your feet touch the top of the mountain. Walk down the mountain path again until you reach the meadow where you started your journey.

Record what you experienced during your visualisation:

Abstract

TRANSFORM YOUR WEALTH – SPIRITUAL AND MATERIAL

Abundance means flowing with love, prosperity, happiness and health and absolutely knowing that more will flow into our life. The Source is unlimited. We draw from Source according to Spiritual Law. The Spiritual Laws are universal so the same principles apply, whether we are drawing to us happiness, prosperity, success, love or health.

Take love. In the Universal Mind there is unlimited abundance. Can you imagine a rich, generous, loving father wanting his children to be poor, sick and unhappy? Of course not. The Universe wants us to be happy, healthy and rich. It wants us to receive. The blockage is at our end.

The only thing that stops us receiving abundance from the Source and from each other is our belief that we don't deserve it. Many of us have pretty low expectations about how much we deserve when someone offers us compliments or money or gifts. We feel embarrassed about receiving. Alternatively we may be greedy or grasping or feel we want more. This is the opposite reaction which comes from the fear that there won't be enough for us.

In either case our attitude blocks the flow. The Universe receives the message that we don't want abundance and stops sending it, whatever form it is in – money, healing abilities, gifts and talents, beauty or anything else.

When we give and receive with joy, abundance must flow through

our lives. The Law of Karma says, as you give so you receive. So everything we send out comes boomeranging back and hits us. This means that what we wish for another we get back ourselves. So envy and jealousy block our own abundance. And generous wishes of good fortune to a rival open us up to opportunity and success.

Under the Law of Karma we get what we expect and not what we wish for. If we want love but expect rejection, we get rejection. If we want to be happy but expect to be miserable, we get the misery. So start expecting good things by imagining them, affirming them and focusing on them.

When we start affirming that we deserve the best, we open ourselves to receiving the best. When we happily receive compliments about our looks, our ability, our lovability, we become more beautiful, more able and more love flows into our lives.

When we can give genuine compliments, be happy to give generously and wish others good fortune, we open our hearts. As we open up, abundance grows from a trickle to a torrent.

We can all have abundance. It is subject to Spiritual Law just like everything else in the Universe.

A powerful ritual is to sit with your arms open, so your heart centre is open, and affirm that you are ready to open to abundance.

1 Over the next few days record how you receive compliments about every area of your life. Start noticing if you have even been hearing them.
   Record what you learn:

_____

_____

(Now make positive efforts to give and receive.)

2 *Draw* a mandala (a circle) and fill it with symbols of abundance:

Prosperity

The Source is a vast unlimited pool of prosperity. We draw from it according to our level of prosperity consciousness. In other words we draw into our lives what we believe we deserve.

Most of us have scarcity consciousness beliefs which block our prosperity. These are beliefs such as, 'If I have more there is less for someone else', which are based on a misunderstanding of Spiritual Law. We all create our own personal reality and attract from the great universal pool quite automatically according to our beliefs.

The belief that we must save for a rainy day focuses our attention on the rainy day. We attract what we focus on and create negative karma. It takes the same amount of energy to focus on positive pictures and prosperous thoughts as it does on scarcity.

Having a reasonable bank balance is great. But when we hoard money out of terror that we won't have enough, we are creating a stagnant pool. Nothing is flowing out and we are giving the Universe the message we don't want prosperity.

We receive our level of deservingness. In order to increase our levels of prosperity, we can decide what we do want and visualise ourselves receiving it. When we pass a beautiful house we can state, 'I deserve a house as nice as this one and am ready to receive it', or decide what job we want and start visualising ourselves being offered it. At the same time we prepare ourselves to be able to do the job.

In order to be prosperous we have to be able to let money flow in with love and we also have to let it flow out with love. As we give so we receive. Most of us give freely to our children or loved ones. But how do we give to the tax man? How do we feel about paying our TV licence? What is in our mind as we write the cheques for the bills?

When we pay with joy at the outflow, then we are open to the inflow. This is Universal Law.

People say that money is the root of all evil. In fact the quotation is: 'Love of money is the root of all evil'. When we concentrate on the material world to the exclusion of the spiritual, then we live limited lives.

Money is a vibration which we can call to us. What we do with it, and how we feel about it, is what lowers or raises our consciousness.

Prosperity can being freedom or power to use in the service of light. Money is a responsibility which gives us opportunities for growth.

Prosperity is a state of mind. We can be more prosperous with one pair of shoes, knowing that the Universe will provide us with another when we need it, than if we have a hundred pairs of shoes and are worried that there won't be any more.

When we flow with prosperity consciousness we touch other people so that they feel safe about money. We raise their consciousness too.

1 What limiting beliefs about money were you brought up with? They are untruths. Write the truth next to each one. For instance, 'You can't be rich and happy.'/'I can be prosperous and very happy.'

_____   _____

_____   _____

2 Start making statements to the Universe about deserving more. Go into a better-quality coffee bar. Buy a more expensive item, even if it is only a few pence. Walk in a better part of town and enjoy the houses. Look at better cars and affirm that you deserve one. Pay with a smile.

Record what you do:

_____

_____

Manifestation

We all manifest things. Everything that is in our lives is there because we have manifested it, consciously or unconsciously.

The Laws which govern manifestation are clarity and faith. If we are clear about what we want, and we hold that vision unwaveringly in our minds, it must come about.

We are all very powerful beings and we can make things happen. It is important that we manifest for the highest good of all concerned. Otherwise we create karma which has to be paid for.

So it is appropriate for us to meditate and listen to our inner wisdom in order to bring things into our lives in accordance with our highest purpose.

Sometimes people are certain that they are clear about what they want, but it doesn't happen. The truth is that they are not clear or they would already have it.

I worked with a woman who said she was clear she wanted to get rid of her life-long asthma and manifest good health. She claimed the asthma served no useful purpose in her life. As we worked she began to get insights about how it served her. She got attention from it. It got her out of doing certain things. It meant that many of her needs were met. In the end she said she'd like to go away and think about it as she didn't think she was ready to give it up yet.

We think we want promotion, a big house, lots of money, but if we look at an unconscious level we find we are not ready for the responsibility involved or we find we hold beliefs which stop it manifesting. When we find the blocking beliefs we can start to change them.

In order to find our blocking beliefs, we may need to visualise ourselves receiving what we think we want and be aware of the fears and doubts which come to mind. They all need to be dealt with.

If we think our abundance means asking for someone else's job or house, then we create karmic repercussions. So we ask for a house equally as attractive or a job as good as or better . . . We ask for it to come to us in a harmonious way for all concerned.

The Law of Prayer is very similar. It says: ask, believing, and it is already granted. So we ask for what we want and, as long as we have total

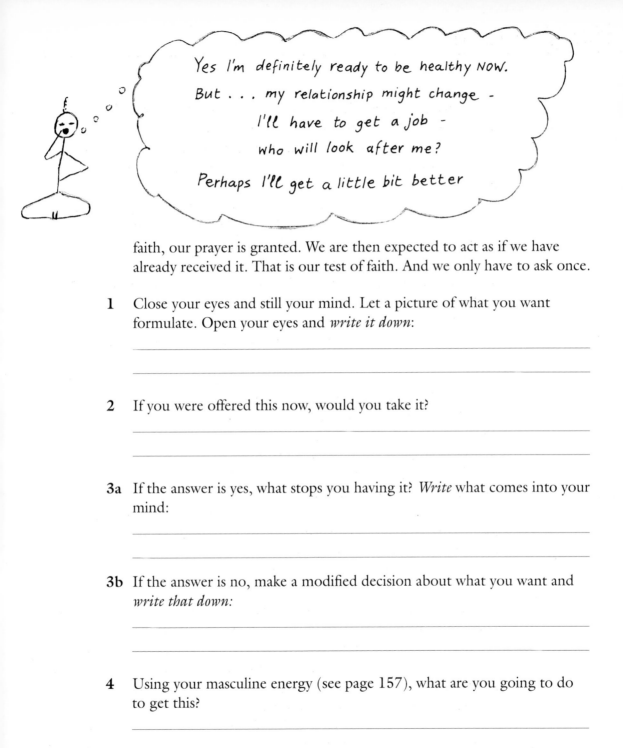

Yes I'm definitely ready to be healthy NOW.
But . . . my relationship might change -
I'll have to get a job -
who will look after me?
Perhaps I'll get a little bit better

faith, our prayer is granted. We are then expected to act as if we have already received it. That is our test of faith. And we only have to ask once.

1 Close your eyes and still your mind. Let a picture of what you want formulate. Open your eyes and *write it down*:

_____

_____

2 If you were offered this now, would you take it?

_____

_____

3a If the answer is yes, what stops you having it? *Write* what comes into your mind:

_____

_____

3b If the answer is no, make a modified decision about what you want and *write that down*:

_____

_____

4 Using your masculine energy (see page 157), what are you going to do to get this?

_____

_____

Visualisation to gain abundance and prosperity

Go to a quiet place where you can be undisturbed. You may like to record this visualisation onto a tape or ask a friend to read it to you.

Close your eyes and breathe comfortably until you feel relaxed.

See in front of you anyone you are in rivalry with or who you don't feel generous or giving towards. Know in your heart that there is enough for everyone and see them receiving exactly what they want. Applaud them. Feel happy for them. Put energy into feeling good for them. They are you in another body.

Now see yourself receiving exactly what you want. Enjoy it. See everyone being happy for you. Know that you deserve it.

Notice that there are people queuing for water. How long is the queue? How do the people look . . . eager and expectant, depressed and miserable? Are they smart or dishevelled? Orderly or wild?

Where is the supply coming from? How big is your container? When you get to the front do you fill it up? What do you do with it then?

Look round and see if there are any other supplies of water, any other channels.

There is a mountain nearby. Climb up to the very top. At the top you find a beautiful waterfall, sparkling in the sunlight. The water comes from a limitless source. Drink your fill.

Notice that the water is flowing with hearts for love, stars for success, keys for opportunity, gold coins for prosperity. It is a never-ending supply. Open up and gather all you want.

You are connected to the supply. Feel the hearts, stars, keys and coins flowing through you to others. The water is flowing through them to others until everyone is touched with your flow of abundance.

Promise the Source that you will now be a channel for the abundance of the Universe.

When you are ready, open your eyes.

Record what you experienced during your visualisation:

_____

_____

Visualisation to release your vision

Find your quiet and undisturbed space and make sure you have enough time to do this exercise. You may like to record this visualisation on to a tape or ask a friend to read it to you.

Close your eyes and relax. With each outbreath let go of tension and negative thoughts. Then focus on your inbreath and take in golden breaths of love and wisdom.

When you feel filled with love and wisdom, think about your vision. Ask the source if it is right for you now or if it needs to be modified.

Make your mind quiet and still by visualising a golden ball behind your physical eyes or imagine yourself walking by a clear, shimmering stream in a green forest. After a few minutes allow your mind to come back to the original vision and sense if it is right for you now. If you feel it needs changing, do whatever needs to be done.

Then picture your true vision in detail as clearly as you can. Feel it manifesting. Put as much emotional energy as you can into enjoying what you have made happen.

Imagine this vision being placed in a balloon. Hold the string and see it blowing above your head. Then let go of the string, symbolically letting go of any attachment to your vision. Say or think: 'This or something better now manifests in a perfect way.'

Watch the balloon sailing up over the countryside, going ever higher into the blue sky. Watch it becoming smaller and sense it attracting the attention and energy of the Universe. Finally it goes out of sight.

Let yourself relax happily for a few moments and then open your eyes and return to the room.

Draw your vision in a pink or golden balloon. Put in as much detail as possible. The more precise you are, the clearer you make your intention to the Source. Write underneath it: 'This or something better now manifests for the highest good of all concerned.'

The body

Our consciousness builds our physical bodies. If our thoughts and emotions are happy, positive and loving we build bodies which are flexible, firm and healthy. Healthy beliefs create healthy bodies.

Where our beliefs are inflexible or negative we build blocks into our bodies. So when we are ill at ease we create disease.

Our bodies never lie. They directly reflect what is really going on in us at an unconscious level. This is one reason why life on earth is so sought after. It is a plane of existence where thoughts and emotions crystallize into physical form, so we have every opportunity to look at them.

Where we hold part of the body in tension, the blood, oxygen and energy cannot reach it and we create a block. Wherever there is such a blockage, a physical manifestation will eventually occur.

When we are angry, blood churns to the part of the body where we hold the feelings. If we don't express the feelings, the energy has no outlet and over time manifests as dis-ease in the physical body.

Anger creates things that burn or boil or become red. It causes infections, inflammations and anything ending in '-itis'.

If we are irritated by something or someone and are either unconscious of it or are not doing anything to change the situation, our body will draw it to our attention by giving us something that itches. Skin rashes, eczema, spots and insect bites may be indicative of this.

If we feel guilty, however unconscious it is, we will cause ourselves pain or somehow punish ourselves. Many an accident happens around times of divorce, redundancy or separation because we feel guilty. 'If I had been a better person this wouldn't have happened . . . '

When we are very afraid, we withdraw our energy from the part of the body where we hold the fear. If we are afraid to move forward we get cold feet. And this same principle applies to all our internal organs. When no blood reaches a part of our body, no oxygen gets there either. We form an energy block. In the short term we may shiver, shake, tremble, quiver or be unable to move with fear. If we hold this same fear for long enough and deeply enough, it will crystallise into a disease with symptoms of paralysis or trembling.

When we are emotionally confused about something, we retain fluids in that part of the body where we hold the confusion. This causes swelling. Maybe we are confused about what we are seeing in our lives and our eyes swell up. Perhaps we are confused about which direction to go in and our ankles swell. Premenstrual tension is often accompanied by swelling, indicating confused thinking about our role as a woman.

Go through your life from babyhood to the present and *write down* all the physical problems you have had, including accidents and illnesses. Write down the part or parts of the body affected and which side of the body you had the problem in. Then write against each one which emotion you think was at the root of the problem. For example:

2 years . . . asthma . . . chest and lungs . . . L and R . . . fear

6 years . . . broke R leg . . . fear of Dad leaving home

_____

_____

_____

Building the body

Every part of our bodies gives us information about ourselves. So wherever something physical manifests we have an opportunity to look at it and grow.

The first thing we build is our skeleton, which forms the framework for our body. Our bones represent our core beliefs, so our skeleton is the expression of the spiritual being we are in this life.

If we have an extreme trauma in childhood we may grow a tall thin body in an effort to grow away from our feelings. If our main spiritual lesson in this life is to deal with our sexuality, we will build ourselves a short square body. At an inner spiritual level we may need to build ourselves an imposing giant frame to deal with life's lessons. Or we may best express our essence by building a small, whippy body to house our active, thrusting, quick-thinking nature.

So if we break a bone it represents a very profound split or conflict within us. When we break a bone we get attention, are looked after and are forced to rest. Perhaps our beliefs wouldn't allow us to get these needs met in any other way. Breaking a bone chiefly indicates a need to make a deep inner change.

We can ask ourselves if we have built ourselves a straight skeleton. Are we a straight person? Do we stand up for our rights? In other words

How do you build your body?

do we have courage and strength and walk with our head held high? Or are we bent? Do we bow our head? Were we beaten into submission or do we feel bad or humbled?

We clothe our bones with our thoughts and emotions. When we have twisted, tense, rigid thoughts, we knot, sprain or tense our muscles. Conversely, strong, flexible, happy thoughts build strong muscles.

Fat is fear. If we stop flowing and resist experiences we put on weight. Where we build tight, firm fat, it indicates deep fear and entrenched mental patterns. Where we have floppy, wobbly fat, it indicates a holding back of emotions, perhaps holding back unshed tears. Where we put it indicates the nature of our fear – our thighs are our past, hanging on to old stuff from childhood or even past lives. Our hips protect our sexuality or indicate a fear of moving forward. Putting on a tummy indicates a need to protect ourselves sexually or emotionally. Big shoulders indicate that we feel we have to carry a lot of burdens. Big arms may indicate a desire to be held and loved, which we never allowed to happen. Big breasts are often a need to over-nurture to compensate for our own lack of nurturing.

The opposite, extreme thinness, indicates a refusal to allow ourselves to be nurtured. There is an underlying feeling of being undeserving or unlovable.

Our tendons link the bones of our core self and the mental energy of our muscles. Unbending attitudes make for stiff, rigid bodies, while flexible attitudes create flowing bodies.

Similarly, if we are afraid to make moves, or are rigid and inflexible about changing our lives or attitudes, our joints stiffen. If our mental set is adaptable so that we can make changes and move forward with ease, our joints move freely.

Draw your skeleton as you imagine it. Note any breakages or stiff parts. Then add the body you have built for yourself. As you draw, let any insights come to consciousness and *note them down*:

_____

_____

Body fluids

Body fluids represent emotions. Urine is the fluid in which we pass waste out of our bodies and it contains the negative emotions we are releasing. When we hang on to old anger, or if we cling to inappropriate sexual beliefs, we create inflammations or infections in the bladder. Cystitis occurs most often at times of difficulty in relationships.

Blood represents the flowing of joy and love through the body. If the blood clots, as in thrombosis, it indicates that we are somehow blocking the giving and receiving of love. Perhaps we are holding on to what is safe and not moving on to the next stage. When we are anaemic our blood is thin and love and joy may be a bit thin in our lives. We need to start loving ourselves more and have some fun.

If we haemorrhage, we are feeling unloved and the emotions are flooding out. We may have felt a long-term lack of love in our lives or we may have moved into a new relationship and this allows all the old pain from an old relationship to come flooding out. Nose-bleeds often indicate that we are feeling unappreciated, out of place and unrecognised.

When we have felt angry and unloved for a long time, we send blood pounding round our arteries and the negative emotions silt them up. So high blood pressure indicates that there has been a long-term emotional build-up and we need a great deal of loving and nurturing to heal ourselves.

Excessive sweating indicates a fear response to a situation. It is a release of emotions. Never sweating, on the other hand, indicates a shrinking away from the problem and withdrawal into the self.

Our lymph glands are the dustbins which clean up the dead cells and rubbish in our bodies. The lymph is the clear fluid which runs through our bodies, constantly purifying us. Swollen glands and a blocked lymph system indicate blocked, poisonous or confused emotions. If they don't work for a long time then our immune system breaks down and we are vulnerable. In this case we have to see what toxic thoughts and attitudes have caused the blockage and made us vulnerable.

If we block tears of grief, sadness or joy our bodies will express them in another way. The runny nose and streaming eyes of a cold, sinusitis or hay fever are often a way to cry acceptably.

A drying up of saliva in the mouth can indicate a fear of taking in nourishment or perhaps a fear of asking for our needs to be met. It may even be a fear of speaking out.

If a man feels sexually ill at ease with his partner he may not be able to ejaculate, in other words to let go emotionally. Likewise, a woman may be dry. Because she is not sexually or emotionally aroused, her sexual fluids do not flow.

1 When was the last time you had a cold, hay fever or sinus problems? What was going on emotionally in your life at that time?

2 If you are a woman, what are your periods like? Do they flow freely and painlessly or do you have swellings and pain? What is going on for you emotionally as a woman?

3 Do you have any problems with flowing sexually?

4 Do you have nose-bleeds, bleeding gums, ulcers or any other form of blood loss other than menstruation? Do you have high or low blood pressure? What could this represent in your emotional life?

The sides of the body

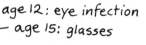

age 12: eye infection
age 15: glasses

age 15: sore throats
age 16: bronchitis

age 17:
twisted ankle

When we are trying to trace the mental or emotional source of a physical problem, the side of the body where it occurs offers helpful clues.

The left side of the body is to do with our *yin* energy. Anything that is dis-eased on this side of our body is to do with women in our lives. So it could relate to mothers, sisters, wives, aunts, daughters, female friends or colleagues. Or, if we are a woman, it could be a blockage in our belief about ourselves as a woman or about women in general.

For either sex, the left side is also to do with the spiritual side of our nature. Perhaps we are holding back our healing ability or our intuition, or maybe we are not allowing ourselves to express our caring, nurturing energy. We could also be holding on to past fears.

The right side is to do with our *yang* energy. Anything that is dis-eased on this side of the body is to do with men in our lives such as fathers, brothers, sons, husbands, male friends or colleagues. Again, for men, it could be a blockage about our belief in ourselves as men or, for women, it could be to do with negative beliefs we hold about men in general.

The yang energy is to do with our career, how we move forward in life, what we do. It is our logical, linear, thinking, aggressive energy which covers money, success, prosperity and how we relate to the outside world.

Every part of our body indicates something specific and it is helpful to have more understanding of this in our quest to transform our consciousness and heal our bodies.

So, for instance, if our right eye became inflamed, we could ask ourselves what we were seeing in our life that we were angry about to do with men or careers. We might realise that we were furious with our boss for blocking our career. This awareness would indicate that it is time for us to do something about the situation.

Our legs are what we stand on. They are what we move forward on and if we injure our left leg, maybe we feel very unstable about a woman in our life or our role as a woman. If we break the left leg, it indicates a much deeper trauma. Maybe a woman we love has died or withdrawn from us. Perhaps we need to make a break with the past? Maybe we want to become a healer and dare not do so, to the extent that we give up? We are literally left without a leg to stand on.

Organ language tells us most of what we want to know. If someone complains about a sore neck, just ask, 'Who's being a pain in the neck?' They will invariably respond with the answer they are looking for.

1 *Draw* a picture of your body. Draw red dots on the right side of your body where you have had problems. Then draw blue dots on the left side of your body where you have had problems.

_____

_____

2 Notice if any pattern emerges. Is there any person or situation that you clearly need to deal with?

What are your options for changing the situation? Remember that when we take a decision in strength to change a situation, however impossible it seems, the universe will support us.

_____

_____

There is a solution for every problem. It is only because of our limited concepts that we believe we are stuck.

Creative visualisation allows us to expand our limitations so that new possibilities can enter our consciousness. We think these colourful ideas are merely imagination. However, imagination is the building block of creation. A building starts with a picture in the architect's mind. Freedom, a healthy body, miracles, all start with a picture in our mind.

When we find a creative solution for a block in the body, the energy flows again and we are healed.

Find a time and place where you can be at ease. Sit or lie down and allow your body to become relaxed. Focus your mind on your breathing until it is quiet. You may like to record this visualisation on to a tape or ask a friend to read it to you.

Let your eyes close. Imagine the picture of your body which you have just drawn and focus on a dot or group of dots.

As you look at the dots you will be able to see a person or situation or symbol come out of that place. Allow the source of the problem to float into your awareness. It may be totally unexpected, so stay open and receptive to all the suggestions that your unconscious mind is producing for you.

Put the picture you have received into a bubble and allow it to go right out into the Universe. Once out there, you can dissolve it in golden light. If you wish you can let it explode into a million pieces.

Now creatively visualise a perfect solution to your problem. Remember that all things are possible. Use all your imagination and ingenuity.

If something that you imagine will be unpleasant for someone else, see a lovely solution for them too. For example, if you want more freedom, which means an old relative going into a home which they don't want to do, visualise them going really happily and being surrounded by friends. There is always a perfect answer.

If you want someone or something which belongs to someone else, this creates bad karma. So if you desire someone who is already attached, imagine someone equally attractive, perfect for you and single coming into your life. If you want something owned by someone else, again imagine something similar or better coming to you.

After you have pictured your vision and perhaps drawn

create a solution

it, say or write: 'This or something better is now coming to me in a perfect way' and add 'Let Thy will be done.'

Miracles happen every day. They are a result of us sending out the right energies to make them happen. Create your own now in your imagination. Put as much emotion and energy into your fantasy as possible. Use all your senses . . . smell, hearing, touch. The more you put into it, the more real you make it.

When you have found a creative solution for everyone, open your eyes and feel happy.

Record or draw your perfect solution, with everybody happy:

_____

_____

Nerves, hair and eyes

Our head indicates the self. It is the control centre for the whole body. From here the commands which run the body are issued.

When we injure our head, or keep knocking it, it indicates a frustration with the self and with our situation. Babies who bang their heads in frustration are often saying that they don't want to be here on Earth. Their memory banks are still open to where they have come from and they would much rather be in spirit.

We often get headaches when we try too hard, usually because we don't believe we are good enough. And if we have low self-esteem, we criticise ourselves and drive ourselves until we get migraines. If we are too much in the head, worrying, thinking, cogitating all the time, we can give ourselves overload headaches.

NERVES   This is our alarm system. The nerves are constantly communicating messages to every part of the body, so if we have a problem with a damaged nerve it would seem that our communications have broken down. Who aren't we communicating with? What aren't we communicating? Is there something within ourselves we are not in touch with?

HAIR   Our hair indicates our thoughts and therefore our strength. Is our hair wild, frizzy and undisciplined, or lank and weak, or shining and healthy, or neat and controlled? When our hair falls out it indicates a fear that we can't cope with some aspect of life. Constant worrying thoughts cause our scalps to tense so that nourishment is cut off from the roots and they die. Baldness tells us that worry is undermining our strength.

EYES   Our eyes are the windows of our soul. If someone doesn't meet our eyes we know, albeit unconsciously, they are lying. When we have eye contact with someone, we are meeting them soul to soul.

If we are near-sighted, we may fear the future. If we are long-sighted, we may be an outgoing personality who doesn't like looking at intimate relationships and things close to us.

Cataracts would indicate that our future appears uncertain to us so

We are all different!

we cloud our vision over. With glaucoma there is a build-up of pressure. Emotions have been building up and we can only see a very narrow pathway ahead of us. Astigmatism suggests that our reality is or was quite uncomfortable, so we try to distort our picture of reality.

1 What shape is your head and body?

A square shape with a short body indicates an earth person, solid, grounded and dealing with earth matters and sexuality in this life.

A round face with a tall body indicates a water personality, dealing with emotions in this life.

An oval face with a small body indicates a fire person, visionary and enthusiastic, learning to keep a sense of perspective.

An oval face with a tall body indicates an air person, often a person of lofty ideals and head in the clouds, needing to keep grounded.

Decide which of these you are, or which mixture you are, and *write* what this indicates for you:

_____

2 What does your hair tell you about your strength?

_____

3 What do your eyes tell you about how you see life? Remember that we all see selectively.

_____

Ears, nose and mouth

EARS Our ears represent how we hear things around us. If we don't like what we hear, and we can't get away from it, we may withdraw into deafness, temporary or permanent. I have literally felt wax running into my ears, blocking them so that I couldn't hear until I had them syringed!

If we are angry or irritated by what we hear, we may develop an ear infection. Children who are unable to escape conflict at home or at school may develop inflammation in their ears.

Tinnitus, which is ringing in the ears, is the mind's way of drowning out things we don't want to hear. It may also be that we are not listening to our inner voice, the voice of our Higher Self.

NOSE Our nose represents our intuition and therefore our sense of who we are. When it gets blocked we may not be listening to our intuition or we may feel we are not being recognised. A runny nose is an acceptable way to cry if we can't express our feelings openly. Sneezing or blocked sinuses suggest that we are irritated by someone. Who is it? And of course nose problems could indicate that we are being nosy!

MOUTH Our mouth is where we take in emotional nourishment in the form of food. We also express ourselves through our mouth. Mouth problems could indicate that we are speaking ill of someone – 'bad-mouthing' them. Or that what is going on in our life is leaving a bad taste in our mouth. Our mouth is a very sensitive, intimate area. Mouth ulcers could indicate that we are being eaten away by lack of love, or not wanting to take in what is going on in our lives.

TEETH Our teeth are used to bite and chew. They symbolise how we speak or how we chew over a problem. Rotting or infected teeth indicate a need to purify what we say or think. Do we gossip unkindly? Teeth are symbolic of decisions, so if we have loose teeth or aching teeth, are we unable to make decisions or do we agonise over them? The gums hold the teeth in place, so problems here indicate being indecisive.

LIPS Kissing is a very intimate form of closeness and lip sores prevent this closeness. What are we sore about? Is closeness difficult for us? Do we feel guilty about enjoying so much closeness?

Lips express emotions and we may have had to hold back and keep a stiff upper lip. What are we holding back now?

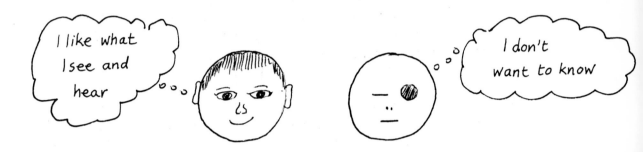

1 *Draw* your face:

2 Have you missed any features out? What does this indicate? For instance, if you missed out ears do you listen to yourself and others? If you missed out eyes how do you see?

3 From what you have drawn and read, what does your head tell you about yourself?

Jaw, neck and throat

JAW When we clench our teeth with anger we clamp down our jaw. This indicates that we are holding on tight and controlling everything. We are afraid to speak in case we change things for the worse. Perhaps we are too afraid of what we might say if we let go. To release this tension we need to be able to express our feelings honestly.

It can help to talk aloud to a cushion, pretending it is the person we want to talk to. Or we can start the process by writing all our feelings down on a piece of paper, then burning it.

If we let tetanus in, it would suggest that we are holding our anger in tightly.

NECK This is what connects the head, our thinking process, with the heart, our feelings. A long neck can indicate a split between the body and the mind, or at least a desire to separate from our feelings. If we appear to have no neck we may have difficulty integrating our thoughts and feelings.

Stiff necks indicate that we are being stubborn, inflexible or proud about something. There is always another point of view. If we could allow ourself to understand the other point of view, what would it be? When we have a pain in the neck we should ask who or what is a pain in the neck? The answer is usually glaringly obvious!

THROAT The throat is very sensitive and this is where we hear our inner guidance. It blocks off if we don't speak our truth. If we get a frog in our throat, or need to clear it, we can be certain we are not speaking our truth or are concerned that what we are saying will not be accepted by others.

If we swallow anger, hurt or disappointment we may develop sore throats. What are we sore about? What do we really want to say? Who do we need to speak to? What is it that we can't swallow?

Throat problems indicate a fear of speaking out. Sometimes we tell ourselves it is for fear of hurting someone but in reality our fear is for ourselves. So what's sticking in our throat? What's strangling us? What are we choking on or being choked by?

If we are very angry, and are afraid that we may say something which will lose us our job or relationship, we may lose our voice. This is our unconscious mind trying to protect us from danger. If we could have spoken, what would we have said and to whom?

1 Sit with a cushion in front of you. Imagine it is a person and talk to it. Express all the things you would like to say if it was the real person. It doesn't matter if he's alive or dead.

When you have finished, swap places and become the other person. Talk from his point of view and really listen and try to understand.

At the end hug the cushion.

What did you want to say and what did the other person want to say to you?

2 How differently do you feel about the relationship or situation and how different does your body feel?

Back

Our back is our support system. It is also where we put things behind us so that we can't see them or deal with them. Who or what do we want to turn our back on? Who is on our back and who do we want off our back?

SPINE   Our spine is our backbone, which indicates courage, stamina, assertiveness. Our kundalini energy, which is our life force, flows through it, so if we have no backbone we are very wishy-washy. If our spine is curved or out of alignment our life force cannot be clearly and strongly expressed.

UPPER BACK   This part of our back lies behind the heart centre and problems here indicate anger or fear that we are not being loved or emotionally supported as we would like to be. It can also indicate that we are wanting to let go of people or situations that we have been carrying.

MIDDLE BACK   This is the part behind the solar plexus, where we hold our self-esteem and self-worth. Problems here indicate that the old guilts, angers and power struggles are holding us back. It is time to raise our consciousness and lift our thought patterns so that the energy can move up to the spiritual.

LOWER BACK This relates to how we feel supported emotionally and financially by the Universe. This is our survival area. If we feel threatened – e.g. we've lost our job, can't pay the mortgage, our relationship has broken down, someone we relied on is ill – our lower back will take the strain. We can be outwardly secure, but still fear something will be taken away. Lower back problems imply a need for inner security.

SLIPPED DISC Here there is an inner conflict about a core issue. Are we pressurising ourselves or is someone or something outside us pressuring us?

OSTEOPOROSIS This is where we feel that our emotional support system is crumbling.

RICKETS We are not receiving enough nourishment to build a strong framework for life.

1 Have you had any back problems? If so, in which part of your back? What was happening in your life in the weeks and months preceding the onset of the problem?

_____

_____

2 Close your eyes. Let the part of your back that is hurting have a voice. Let it tell you how it feels. Listen sympathetically and encourage the voice to say anything it wants to. Don't censor it or divert it. Simply listen and allow the voice to express what it has wanted to for a long time. When it has completely finished, agree to help it in some suitable way.

So if your back tells you that it's fed up with carrying your complaining friend and you are standing too long in high heels, make a deal with it on the emotional and physical levels. Let go of your friend and buy some new shoes.

Record the information your back gives you:

_____

_____

Shoulders, arms and hands

SHOULDERS We carry our responsibilities and burdens on our shoulders. This is where we carry the decisions we have made for this life. Have we built ourselves sloping shoulders, implying that we are not willing to shoulder responsibility or burdens? They slip off sloping shoulders.

Or have we created square solid shoulders ready to carry lots of responsibility? Sometimes we build huge great shoulders, which suggests that we feel that we have weighty things to carry, so we'd better be prepared. It is an armouring because we don't really want to bear it all. Hunched shoulders say that we don't want to have to deal with things.

A frozen shoulder indicates that the flow from the heart has frozen up with the hurt of rejection. We may feel we have been given the cold shoulder, maybe by someone dying or leaving us. We can ice up a shoulder if our womanhood or manhood has been insulted. Perhaps we want to give someone the cold shoulder?

ARMS Our arms are a direct extension of the heart energy. When we open our arms to someone, we open our heart centre. So the arms indicate the ability to reach out and embrace life or people or situations.

Weapons are an extension of our arms. To carry arms suggests that we are ready to fight in order to defend ourselves or to attack.

So arms can indicate how we embrace life or how we attack it. If we can't use an arm, what would we do with it if we could?

ELBOWS Our elbows can give grace to the expression of our arms or they can be bony and awkward. Problems here indicate difficulty with changing our ideas about life. Or who do we want to elbow out? Who's elbowing us out? Do we have to put in too much elbow grease?

Tennis elbow is an inflammation of the tendon which indicates difficulty in making moves, mental, emotional or physical. It is very painful, so perhaps we are feeling guilty about wanting to make moves?

HANDS Hands express how we handle life. With hands we give and receive, so if we have problems we can ask: are we being tight-fisted or open-handed? Are we clutching and holding on? Who is cramping our style? Do we have

cold hands so that our heart energy doesn't reach what we are doing? Are our hands hot and sweaty, indicating that we're pouring too much emotion into what we are doing? Our hands touch, stroke, applaud. How do we feel about doing these things?

FINGERS   Fingers express how we deal with the details of life.

1   Look at your arms and hands. Are they graceful and flowing or awkward? Practise graceful movements with your arms and hands. Make the movements bigger and more expansive, so that the heart energy flows right down into the fingers. Making big sweeping movements with your arms expands and energises your aura.
    Note how it feels. Where in your body feels different?

_____

_____

2   Where in your shoulders, arms or hands do you have a problem? Close your eyes and focus on the problem area. What does it feel like? Is it tight, tense, throbbing? Does it feel like stabbing pain or aching? Listen to the message of the sensation. The ache in your shoulder may be saying that you are aching to be looked after. The stiffness in your arm may be saying you'd like to beat someone if you could move it. Stay open and receptive to your unconscious.
    Record your impressions:

_____

_____

Chest, heart and lungs

CHEST Our chest is the front that we show the world. It protects our heart centre which houses our feelings and emotions, our secrets, longings, hopes and desires. We may puff out our chests to pretend we are more powerful than we feel or put on a good front to cover our inadequacies. We may be tight-chested and afraid to open our hearts or we may build powerful chests to armour our vulnerable hearts.

LUNGS Our lungs indicate our ability to breathe freely or to breathe for ourselves. They express our ability to be independent and self-assured. Problems indicate that we daren't breathe because we are afraid of life or because we are controlled or dominated by someone.

Asthma can say that we are dependent on someone looking after us and we are afraid to breathe for ourselves. We may be being emotionally smothered by someone. Asthma can also indicate unexpressed grief or sobbing which may be many lives deep.

A cough suggests an irritation. What do we want to get off our chest? What do we want to express?

BREASTS We nurture with our breasts. Breast problems can indicate a tendency to over-nurture. This may mean wanting to prove our womanhood or femininity or that we are a good mother. Or we may want to keep people dependent on us so that they won't leave us. We are compensating for the part of us that feels unnurtured. We may also have problems in this area because we feel we ought to nurture others and we don't want to. Either way, cancer of the breast indicates that our needs are not being met, as we feel our role is to meet the needs of others.

Breasts are also the sexual symbol of our womanhood, and conflicts about how we feel as a sexual woman can be expressed in this area of the body.

The left breast expresses our feelings about being a woman, wife or mother and our distress that our needs in this area are not being met, while our right breast expresses our conflicts in life as a woman.

HEART If our heart is open we forgive hurts and slights easily and we are open to the joy of life. But if we hold on to old hurts and harden or clamp down our heart, we create the conditions for heart attacks. Angina indicates that we are squeezing our heart with hurt or perhaps we feel it is too dangerous to be loved. High blood pressure shows that we are feeling under emotional pressure from past hurts or that we feel unloved and want more love.

1 What front do you put on in public? Is your chest puffed out (a brave front) or are you tight-chested (holding your feelings in)?

_____

_____

2 Why have you created this particular protection? What is your underlying fear?

_____

_____

3 Do you have any physical problems in the trunk area? Close your eyes and listen to what that problem part of your body wants to say to you. How can you help this part of your body to feel better?

_____

_____

Visualisation to heal the heart

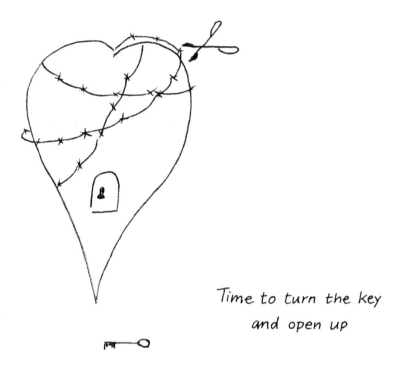

Time to turn the key
and open up

Whether you have physical problems with this part of your body or not, this exercise will bring awareness about your heart centre and help to open it up.

You may like to record this visualisation on to a tape or ask a friend to read it to you.

Close your eyes and relax. Let your eyelids feel heavy and comfortable. Breathe deeply and rhythmically.

When you are relaxed imagine that your heart has been taken out of your body and is in front of you. Is there anything blocking your heart, e.g. barbed wire, hands, a fence? If there is, creatively free the block in any way necessary. Take as much time as you need to do this thoroughly.

How big is your heart? What colour is it? How does it feel?

You are holding a little golden key in your hand. Look carefully and you will find a small door at the side of your heart. Put the key into the door and open it.

Go inside your heart. If necessary put a light on or open windows so that you can explore it thoroughly. Do anything that is required to open it up or clean it. It may need to be washed out or painted.

Now make it warm and welcoming. You may do this symbolically by furnishing it and filling it with flowers, music, beautiful things and a candle or fire . . . or in any way you want.

When it is open, clean, warm and welcoming, go to the door and invite people to come in and greet them warmly.

Allow people to come and go freely. Notice that when your heart is open and welcoming, people enjoy coming in and you are happy to let them come in and to allow them to leave.

When you have completed the exercise put your heart back into your chest and leave the door open so that the love spreads through your body.

Record what you experienced during your visualisation and then *draw* your heart open and welcoming:

_____

_____

Solar plexus

This is where we hold our gut feelings. Our guts relate to personal courage and this is the area where we hold our feelings of self-worth, confidence and self-esteem. It is our power centre.

It is also the place where our spirit can leave our body when we are asleep and if we don't come back in straight for some reason, we can feel pretty sick or disorientated until we have relaxed back in.

STOMACH This is where we digest ideas. How do we stomach things in our life? When we get an upset stomach, is there someone or something we can't stomach? Perhaps we can't stomach the idea of something happening? When we feel empty of love, we try to stuff ourselves with the love substitute, food, especially sugar. This is the basis of obesity. The opposite is anorexia, when we try to control our feeling of not being loved by not letting food (love) in. With bulimia, there is a feeling of desperation. Our confidence and self-esteem is so low that it becomes self-loathing. We stuff ourselves and then reject it by being sick. Underneath we are crying to be loved, nourished and accepted.

If we have an ulcer we can ask what's eating away at us? Is it resentment, hurt, bitter thoughts?

GALLBLADDER If we have problems here, we have usually felt unloved or unvalued in life. When we feel resentful and bitter this will eventually crystallise into a stone.

LIVER The liver is the seat of deep emotions and this is where we hold primitive anger. Problems here indicate that our liver can't cope with all our negative emotions and we need to relax and harmonise our life, especially our relationships.

KIDNEYS Our kidneys filter and cleanse emotions and ideas. That which we no longer need is released. Kidney problems indicate that we are holding on to old emotional patterns. Old griefs and angers we have never been able to express crystallize here and form stones. When they pass, at last, we have been able at one level to let the pain go.

I hold onto the past

bitterness

I enjoy today

joy

BLADDER   The purpose of the bladder is to release old emotions. Problems here suggest that we are holding on to old feelings. Cystitis often occurs when we are feeling negative towards our partner or holding on to deep fears which we can't express.

1 This area is very much to do with holding on to old negative emotions. Addictions and addictive feelings have their roots here. Eating, sex, alcohol, work, talking, spending, exercising, gambling to excess are compulsive forms of behaviour to stop our feelings from surfacing. Any form of extremism can indicate an addiction. If our belief is that we are not safe, or we're not good enough, we will do something to keep these uncomfortable feelings at bay.

Become aware of what you do to excess. For instance, if you become aware that you are addicted to talking, make a determined effort to stop talking and let the uncomfortable feelings surface. Don't edit the thoughts. Accept them. *Record them*:

_____

_____

2 For every negative thought that has surfaced, *write down* a positive one to counteract it:

_____

_____

Lower trunk

THE BOWELS The purpose of the bowels is to eliminate old ideas, concepts, thinking patterns and beliefs. When we have a feeling of insecurity we try to control life, so we hang on to the old worries and problems and become constipated. We cannot forgive and forget because we are frightened to change.

Diarrhoea indicates that we want to get rid of things quickly without looking at and learning from what is presented to us. Alternatively, we may be afraid and wanting to run away.

HIPS Hips express our mobility and adaptability and freedom in life. Old people who see nowhere to move forward to often fall and break a hip.

WOMB This is the inner core of our being where we bring forth new birth. So this indicates an area of new concepts. New ideas from the creative mind take root and develop here.

Problems here come from the fears we hold about the new. Are we afraid of pregnancy or birth? Will we be a good mother? Do we really want to be tied down with children or with a new business or a new idea? When our children grow up do we feel useless, redundant? What does life hold for us now?

VAGINA This is our channel of creativity, through which the new seed is planted. Problems here occur when our creativity is blocked or we have an emotional block about sex. Vaginitis can indicate anger with our partner or guilt about our sexuality or fear of invasion or deep intimacy.

PROSTATE This is closely linked to sexual power and, of course, sexual power is linked with a sense of confidence and personal power. As they become older, many men feel frightened of losing their power. Who are they and what is their function? Men live longer and enter long retirement periods and they are confused about their role. At the same time they are afraid that they will become impotent sexually as well as in business and family life.

TESTICLES All a man's hidden sexual fears are held here. Men may be afraid of losing their sexuality, their potency, their masculinity, their very manhood.

1 What feelings, emotions or material things do you hold on to?

2 Where do you need to forgive?

3 *List* all that you ever heard about the big bad dangerous world:

4 *List* all the prohibitions you ever heard about sex:

5 Copy this page or photostat it or tear it out. Then tear it into little pieces and burn it or flush it down the loo.

FANTASY TO RELEASE INHIBITIONS Find time and space to do this exercise. Close your eyes for a few moments and imagine you have let go of all your inhibitions and fears. Let yourself have a glorious fantasy about what your life could be like. Imagine all sorts of new and amazing experiences opening up to you.

Write your fantasy, how it feels and all that you experience:

free at last

1 Did you enjoy your liberating fantasy? How does your body feel? It may feel tight and tense, free or relaxed. If it feels tight and tense, what do you need to heal the fear? If it feels liberated or relaxed, what are you going to do to change your life? *Write* what comes up for you:

2 *Draw* a picture of the liberated you:

Legs and feet

These are what we stand on. When they are strong we can stand up for our rights and we have the power to go forward towards our goal. If our legs are weak, we may feel we don't have a leg to stand on. If we keep injuring our legs we are possibly feeling undermined or are moving in the wrong direction. We could also ask ourselves: who do we want to kick or what do we want to run away from?

THIGHS   Our thighs protect our sexuality, our masculine or feminine nature. We also hold here deep emotions from our past or deep inner fears.

KNEES   We kneel in submission to the Higher Power, so a problem in our knees could indicate a resistance in this direction; in other words, being stubborn, lacking humility or being inflexible. So knee problems often indicate a stubborn refusal to bend to authority.

   On the other hand, if we are too ready to kneel and humble ourselves we could be indicating a fear of authority or fear of facing something or someone. Our knees tremble or buckle under us when we are afraid.

ANKLES   Our ankles support us and give us flexibility to move in whichever direction we choose. Bruised, sprained or twisted ankles indicate that we don't feel supported. Perhaps we need to take a new direction or we can't cope with a new direction without more support. A broken ankle suggests a much deeper conflict about the direction we move in, especially if our support system has been withdrawn.

FEET   These indicate our foundation. We are solid and independent when we can stand on our own two feet. Then we can put our foot down. It is with our feet that we step forward in life. If we have cold feet, it literally means we are afraid of moving forward. Foot problems suggest that we feel dependent or are not sure which direction to go in.

HEELS   What are you being a heel about? Or who is being a heel to you? Our Achilles tendon is our weak spot, so what do you feel vulnerable about?

TOES These indicate the minor details of life. Do we understand and cope with the small things? Toes help us stay balanced. Do little things knock us off balance? We pull back or curl up our toes as a way of withdrawing from life. What is it we don't want to deal with?

1 What is your goal in life? What is your short-term aim (six months)? What is your long-term goal (five years)?

Short term goal:

_____

_____

Long term goal:

_____

_____

2 What do your legs, knees, ankles and feet tell you about how you are getting to your goals? Are you crawling, walking, running, dancing, racing? Are you supported? Are you going in the right direction? Are you enjoying your journey?
   Write what comes up for you:

_____

_____

3 In order to impress on your unconscious mind that you are now ready to follow a steady path to your goal, *draw* your goal with you heading towards it:

Owning our bodies

Very often in childhood we give part of our body away, either because we let go of responsibility for it or because we feel someone else owns it. If we give part of our body away, we will be out of touch with it. Often we want to destroy it as an alien part of us.

So if our parents were over-controlling about potty training, we may have given responsibility for our bladder or bowel movements to them. This means we may disregard our body's messages, so we hang on until we become constipated or we may empty only half our bladder, opening ourselves to problems, or keep going to the loo unnecessarily.

Where there were emotional problems at home, and food became an issue, we may feel that our parents are in control of our emotions and therefore our stomach.

We may refuse to eat certain foods, starve ourselves, stuff ourselves, eat quickly or slowly, often still unconsciously protesting against Mother or because food and emotions are inextricably woven together. Some people, even as adults, have to finish everything on their plates whether they want to or not. They can say no to other things but not food. Others always have to leave something.

Many of us are so out of touch with our stomachs that we don't even know when we are hungry or we never let ourselves get hungry.

As children, many of us have so many sexual prohibitions put on us that we tie locks and chains around our sexual areas and throw the key away or let one of our parents hold the key. This means that, as adults, we will repress our sexuality or devalue ourselves by giving ourselves away sexually because of a feeling of underlying worthlessness.

If a little girl's hair belongs to Daddy, and her long golden locks symbolise his love for her, she is going to have a problem owning it back for herself and having it cut.

And whatever part of us we have handed over, we need to claim back ownership and take over responsibility for looking after that part.

Where we have dis-ease in our body, there are accompanying sensations which give us clues as to the source of the problem. It is most effective to go to the dis-eased part and listen to what the sensation is trying to tell us.

1 If you are paralysed, what are you paralysed by – rage, fear, jealousy, hurt?

2 If you ache, who or what are you aching for? What are you aching with – loneliness, emptiness or something else? What do you need to satisfy the aching part? Who do you need to hold you?

3 If the disease causes pain, what is the pain like? If it is a stabbing pain, who is stabbing you? What with? If it feels like a red hot poker, who is holding it? Bring up any pictures around it.

4 If you have an infection or inflammation, is it hot? What is the heat like? Does it burn, boil, seethe, scald or catch fire? What do you need to heal yourself?

5 If the disease is cold, is it cool, cold or freezing? Does it feel like cold drizzle or snow or ice?

6 Allergies. Who or what are you allergic to?

Visualisation to heal your body

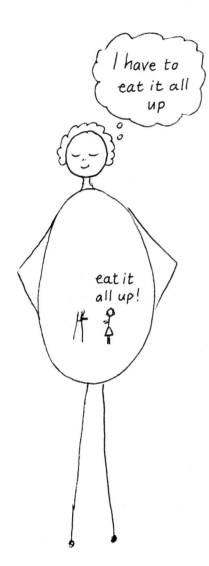

Find a place where you can be quiet and undisturbed for half an hour or so.

You may like to record this visualisation on to a tape or ask a friend to read it to you.

Close your eyes and relax. It is time to breathe deeply and let go. Feel each outbreath relaxing your face. Let it relax your forehead, your eyes, your cheeks, nose and jaw. Then let the breaths relax your body, moving slowly down your front, your back, your arms and legs. Sense yourself floating and feel all your day-to-day worries just dissolving away. They are unimportant at this moment.

Imagine yourself becoming very small. You are so small that you can walk through your mouth. Just spend a moment or two getting the feeling of the tiny you inside your mouth. What does it feel like?

Now you can move to any part of your body you wish to explore. Go to the place where you have a problem. Approach it carefully and sense how it feels as you get closer. Is it hot, boiling, cold, dry, swampy? Is the blood flow restricted or moving too fast? Explore this part of your body and sense what is going on.

What does it need to heal it? Is there something or someone you need to deal with?

Creatively visualise yourself, with any help you need, healing this part of your body.

When this part of your body is completely healed, how are you going to live your life differently so that it stays healthy? See yourself living your life in this new way.

When that part of your body feels comfortable and flowing, move to any other place and repeat the exercise.

Record what you experienced during your visualisation:

_____

_____

Bodymap

Draw a picture of your body. If you have a willing friend and a huge piece of paper, it is even better to lie on the paper and get a friend to draw round your actual body. Give yourself time and space to fill in your bodymap by answering the following questions:

What is your heart like? How big is it? How strong? How happy? What does it want to say to you?

What is your liver like? What colour is it? What anger do you hold here?

Is your body locked anywhere? Or blocked anywhere?

Does part of your body belong to someone else? If you have any troubled organs ask them who owns them?

Are you poisoned by food or drugs?

Mark in any traumas.

Mark in the troubled parts of your body. Who are you punishing with this problem? What payoff does it have? Does it keep you feeling bad about yourself? Does it stop you doing something? What happened in the two years before the trouble started?

Where is your energy now in your body? Are your feet grounded?

Where is the guilt in your body? How big is it?

How big is the anger? Where is it held?

Where do your parents live inside you? How much room do they take up?

Talk to your sexuality. Is it free or locked away? What or who is blocking it? Who owns it?

Talk to your creativity. What has happened to it? If it is not being freely expressed, where is it locked away and how can you release it?

Talk to the stress, fear, hate, guilt, jealousy, success, failure and love and put in a colour, shape or symbol to mark each one.

Notice all the thoughts that have come up. This exercise is only the beginning. It is a trigger for more and more to be released to consciousness. Become aware of what you need to do to heal your life and start to take the necessary steps, lovingly and gently.

Draw your bodymap:

Spontaneous drawings

Spontaneous drawing is like handwriting. Our unconscious minds reveal a great deal about us. We can learn to translate this and bring information to conscious awareness.

Colours are feelings. Clairvoyants have consistently described the colours which appear in our auras and which reflect our feelings. So the colours that we choose are significant and important. The meaning of the colours is listed separately on pages 162–164.

I suggest that you do the drawings first and then refer to the list of colours when you have done them. Be aware that with the act of drawing something happens in our consciousness.

Draw a tree. But, before you do so, cover the rest of this page. Then answer the questions below.

You have drawn yourself. The tree symbolises your life.

Do you have roots? Are they deep enough to get nourishment? Are they strong enough to support you? If not, how can you develop your support system – by making new friends, joining a support group, widening your interests?

Are you in flower, in leaf, evergreen, seasonal, blossoming, fruiting, bare?

Are your branches strong?

Are you flexible, graceful, spiky, rigid? What are you like?

Is there any life nesting or living in you?

Do you shelter anyone?

Are you in sun or shade?

Are you straight or do you lean to right or left?

Are you centred or up in the air?

Are you alone or with other trees?

Is there enough space for you? If you find that you really need to extend beyond the paper, there is potential in you that you are not using at the moment.

How would you like it to be? If you wish to do so, you may now alter your tree with the clear intention of putting messages of change into your unconscious mind.

Drawing a house

Draw a house. A house is symbolic of ourselves. It symbolises who we are, whether we are an open person, whether we have lots of potential and how we feel about life.

Cover up the questions below and look at them when you have finished.

Assume you are the house and answer as if you have drawn yourself.

Are you in the centre of the page or up in the air? Are you too much to the right of the page? The right is the masculine side. It is the thinking, intellectual, career-oriented, doing side of our nature. Or are you too much to the left of the page? The left is our feminine side. It is the passive, nurturing, healing, feeling, intuitive side of our nature. It is the past.

Are you straight and balanced or do you lean?

Are you conventional or unusual? If you are unusual, what is unusual about you?

Are you built on firm foundations?

Are you large or small? This could indicate your body or your consciousness.

Are there lots of rooms in you? Do you have lots of potential?

Are your doors and windows open or closed? Are they big or small? Are you an open or closed person?

Are you in sun or shade? Interpret being in the sun as being happy or appreciated. If you are in shade or cloud, in what way are you unhappy or unappreciated?

Are you alone or are there houses around you? Do you feel crowded or isolated or comfortable?

Is there life in or around you?

Who lives in you? If it is not you, who is it? Has this person taken over your life? How does this person influence you?

Who do you want to welcome in?

Are there any unusual features you want to explore?

Is there anything you want to change?

Drawing yourself

Draw a picture of yourself. It doesn't have to be artistic. It can be a pin figure if you can't draw. Cover up the questions below and look at them when you have finished your self-portrait.

Are you in the centre of the page or up in the air (ungrounded), on the right of the page (the future, the masculine side) or too much to the left (the past, the feminine side)? What is the mood and feeling of the drawing? If you are straight and rigid, how can you free your life and have more fun? If you are tiny and frightened, how can you find help?

Blockages at the *throat* are indicated by neckties, necklaces and high-necked dresses. These indicate that you need to express your feelings. We hold our sexuality in at the waist. If you are belted in or buttoned up here you need to release yourself.

Where we place emphasis, there is a lot of energy. If you draw a double line at the *neck* you probably have neck ache and are being rigid about something. Emphasis round the middle suggests that you are holding your feelings in, emphasis round the jaw that you hold unexpressed anger.

A large *head* indicates that you think a lot. Your hair represents your thoughts. Is it wild, straight, tidy or messy? Have you got eyes? If not, what aren't you seeing? Do you see your own needs? Have you got ears? If not, what aren't you hearing? Do you hear your own needs? Do you have an open mouth? Are you talkative or tight-lipped?

A long *neck* suggests that you may have separated from your feelings; no *neck* that you have difficulty integrating your thoughts and feelings. Are your *shoulders* big, ready to carry responsibility? Or do they slope, indicating that you don't want to carry it? Are your *arms* graceful and welcoming or rigid? Do you have *arms* to reach out? Do you have *hands* to handle life? Are your *breasts and chest* nurturing? Are your *hips* ample or thin? Are your *legs* big and solid, or thin so that they hardly support you? Do you need to ask for more emotional support in life? Are your *feet* pointing in opposite directions? If so, what is your conflict? Are they big enough to support you?

Be aware of what your self-portrait tells you and then decide what you can do about it.

Drawing your parents

No one would ever guess we aren't happy, would they?

Without looking at the questions below, *draw your parents*. Then read the questions which will help you to interpret the drawings.

You have drawn your unconscious interpretation of your feelings about your parents. By adulthood you have internalised your parents, so what you have drawn are your internalised parents. This picture symbolises how you parent yourself. It also tells you how your masculine and feminine energies are working together.

Is one parent more dominant than the other? Which one? If it is the father, in what way does your masculine energy dominate? Are you too left-brain, thinking and calculating, too career-minded or strong or aggressive? If the mother is more dominant, in what ways are you too feminine? Are you too dreamy, always meditating, or very emotional or over-nurturing? How can you balance this out? Be aware that your mother may have been the masculine one in your house and vice versa. If one parent is weak, how does that aspect of you need strengthening? If one parent was controlling, how do you keep control of yourself?

How do your parents look? Happy, warm, loving, open, complete, balanced? Or grim, uptight, inflexible, out of balance? Can you identify these feelings in yourself? What can you do to change this, e.g. have more fun, listen to other people's ideas and viewpoints?

Do your inner parents have eyes, ears, mouths, arms, etc? See page 156. In other words, do you see or hear the needs of your inner child? Do you take care of yourself properly? Is any part of the body missing? How does not having this affect you? Is any part of the body emphasised? For instance, if there are extra lines round the middle, do you hold everything in emotionally? Have you drawn the whole of your parents? If not, perhaps you don't understand them or how they parented you? This means that you don't know how you parent yourself. Are your parents facing towards or away from each other? Is this how you relate to the opposite sex? Do your masculine and feminine aspects work together or against each other?

What would you now like to say to these internalised parents?

How can you strengthen yourself so that you can parent yourself in a wiser, more balanced way?

Drawing your family

Without looking at the questions below, *draw your family*. Draw your parents, brothers, sisters and any other significant family members at a time when you were younger than seven. (Any siblings who are more than seven years younger than you won't appear.)

When you have finished the drawing, look at your family and get a sense of the mood. What does this family need – fun, laughter, consolidation, togetherness? Do you still need this now?

Have you drawn everyone on the same level or are some members of the family placed higher or lower than others? What does this mean? How differently were these particular family members treated and how did this affect you?

Is the family close or not? Are some family members grouped together while others stand apart? Do the siblings separate the parents? Are the parents together while the siblings are apart? How do you feel in this family set up? How do you set these groupings up in your life now?

Have you emphasised any of the family members? What was important for you about this person or people? Or have you emphasised parts of their bodies? For instance, have you drawn your mother with a big mouth (always talking)? Is one of them not joined together (falling to pieces emotionally or physically)? One with a hole in his head (mentally unstable)? How do these things affect you now?

Is there anyone in this group with whom you have unfinished business? What do you need from this person? Allow yourself to talk to them as they are in the picture and complete what you need to.

When we have unfinished business with one person, we continue to attract people into our lives who give us the same feeling as the original person did. Who else do you need to complete with? Imagine yourself now talking to this person and receiving what you need from them.

Look at your drawing. What memories come up for you to deal with?

Drawing symbols

Everything has a symbolic meaning. When we translate a symbol, the first question we ask ourselves is: 'What does this mean to me?' To one person a bee might mean honey, to others it might mean summer, danger, noise and disturbance or being stung! The overriding consideration is our own personal experience.

Certain symbols do have universal meanings and can be interpreted accordingly. As we have seen, a house is our consciousness and a tree represents our life.

For this exercise I suggest you draw five to seven symbols from the following list: a tree, a house, a vehicle, a figure, the sun, water, a flower, a fence, a path, a butterfly, a gate, an animal.

When you have finished your drawing, notice where you have placed your symbols. The right-hand side of the page represents the future or where you are aiming towards or what you can't express, and the left-hand side represents the past or where you are coming from or what you can't let go of. Old attitudes would be placed on the left and so would gifts you are bringing forward.

On another level the left of the page always includes our feminine aspects and the right-hand side, our masculine attributes.

Are there any spaces on the page? A big space on the right could indicate that you don't know where you are moving to in life; on the left or at the bottom, that you don't want to look at your past. A space in the centre might mean that you are feeling empty inside, something in your life needs filling.

A TREE   The tree represents your life. A bare tree on the left of the page might indicate that your past was lifeless, whereas a bare tree on the right would suggest that you see your future as bleak. These could also indicate that your feminine or masculine aspects need some attention. You could, on the other hand, be full of blossom or fruit. A fruiting tree on the right suggests that you have a lot of potential to fulfil. Please refer to page 154 for more details to help you understand your tree drawing.

A HOUSE   This is you, your consciousness. On the left, it could be you in the past, or a way of thinking you are leaving, or childhood experiences you are

159

leaving. On the right, it is the new consciousness you are moving into. For more details to help you understand your house drawing, please refer to page 155.

VEHICLES This represents the way you are moving through life. Are you moving quickly or slowly? A jet plane or a racing car would indicate that you are going fast, whereas a bicycle or a caravan suggests a more leisurely pace. Do you enjoy your mode of transport? Are you carrying any passengers? If you could see them, who would they be? How does this feel? Which direction are you going in? Forward, to the right? Or back into the past to the left to heal something?

A FIGURE Who have you drawn? If it isn't yourself, what does this person mean to you? Have you given responsibility for your life to him or her? Which way is your figure facing? If it is to the left, the past, are you spending too much time looking back in your life? Or are you looking forward to the future, the right? What is the feeling and attitude of this person?

THE SUN This is your power, your force. It is your happiness. Where is it? Is it in the centre of your life, shining right down on you? Or coming from the past? Or shining on to your future? Is it pale yellow, indicating that you think a lot and don't have much power or happiness? Or is it golden (a lot of wisdom)? Or bright orange, indicating that you are really coming into your own? Is any part of it obscured by cloud or anything else? Is it rising? You are moving into your power. Is it setting, indicating an auspicious time when we connect with spirit?

WATER Water represents emotions and also sexuality. Is it clear or murky? Is it flowing? Is it a big or small expanse of water? Does it feel safe to go into? Have you placed anything in it? What could this indicate?

FLOWER This is your essence. It is your creativity, your beauty. What kind is it? Is it common or rare? Is it fragile or strong? What do you feel about this flower? Where are you growing? Are you in a safe place? Is the essence of who you are out in the sun where it can bloom or is it hidden?

FENCE This is your block. What have you blocked off? What can't you get to? Is there a way through? Is the fence in your past or blocking your future? How high is it? What purpose does it serve? If it still affects you, how can you deal with it creatively?

PATH This indicates your path in life. Is it wide or narrow? Straight or crooked? Bumpy or smooth? Is it moving to the right, the future? Or is it going back into the past? This may indicate that you need to go back to heal something or that you keep living in the past. Is your path ahead clear or blocked?

BUTTERFLY A butterfly means transformation or metamorphosis, so it indicates joy, inner beauty and change. How big is your butterfly? Is it flying or resting? Is it on or near any other symbol? What do you feel this means? In which direction is it moving? Forward to the right or back to the left?

GATE This is your opportunity. Is your gate open, indicating that you can move forward now? Or is it barred, closed or half open, showing that you are not ready yet? Is the gate in the fence, indicating that there is a way out of your problem? Or is the gate across your path? Does it stop you or has it stopped you in the past? What does the gate open to?

ANIMAL The animal you have chosen to draw is, of course, an aspect of you. What qualities do you associate with this animal? These are qualities in you. If they are helpful qualities, thank your unconscious mind for drawing them to your attention. If they are negative qualities, you have obviously needed these characteristics in the past to protect yourself. How can you change this now? Where is your animal? Is it in the water, on the path, hiding, coming from the past? What does this tell you about these qualities in you?

Choose some of these symbols and *draw* them. Be aware that your unconscious mind will find a way to bring you information about your life even though you are consciously aware of how to translate some of this information. Go back and draw the symbols you haven't yet done. Ask yourself why you haven't yet drawn these particular symbols.

Choosing colours

The colours we choose are very significant. They represent feelings we hold within us as noted by clairvoyants.

We may have drawn someone a particular colour because they always wear that colour. They wear that colour to express certain feelings and our unconscious mind is now drawing this to our attention.

You may like to have another look at your drawings and glean further information by interpreting the colours you have chosen.

Clear, bright colours indicate that you are positive, grounded and true to your ideals.

Pale pastels indicate immaturity or weakness in that area.

Ethereal colours suggest someone ungrounded, spaced or very aesthetic.

Murky or dingy colours mean there is mental or emotional negativity to deal with.

BROWN *clear brown* earthly, physical, practical, materialistic
dark dull brown depression, inaction, lack of ambition
muddy brown negative attitudes, confusion
greenish brown greed, jealousy, negativity

BLACK suppression and fear, mysterious, unknown, total femininity

GREY mourning, sadness, depression

RED *clear red* energy and vitality
light red same, with less force and maturity
murky red anger, misused energy
dried blood red problems with menstruation, menopause or childbirth

ORANGE friendly, sociable, extrovert, positive ambition

PEACH sensual, combination of the pink of love and the gold of wisdom

YELLOW masculine colour, thinking, in the head
deep yellow inspired, on a mission
gold wisdom
muddy yellow negative thinking, confusion, poor health

GREEN *emerald* genuine service, inner peace, love and balance
avocado/yellow green cowardice, deceit
khaki/dark olive unconscious fears, conforming attitudes
pale green immaturity, sympathy rather than empathy
spring green new growth, healing, vitality
dark green negative and punitive

PINK the heart colour, denoting love
pale pink a need to touch or be touched, looking to safety of babyhood
and wanting to be nurtured
deep pink depth and maturity of love
magenta a breakthrough to higher love

BURGUNDY *rich clear burgundy* prosperity, success, wealth, power
dull or murky selfish

BLUE the female colour, spiritual, loyal, true blue or genuine
turquoise ability to communicate or mediate, honest
light blue can be negative, indicating dependence or spiritual qualities
starting to develop
blue/green spiritual teacher, peaceful, trustworthy
deep blue intuition, healing ability, spiritual, wise

MAUVE *light mauve* spaced, escaping into fantasy
AND *pinky mauve* enlightenment, breakthrough, transformation
PURPLE *purple* high spiritual nature, oneness with God, healing abilities
red purple we offer ourselves but are angry, a martyr or sacrifice

Choosing colours (continued)

VIOLET high spiritual qualities, inspired, religious aspiration, spiritual leader, devotion

WHITE space, openness, purity, new beginnings; are you whitewashing something?

IVORY superiority, purity tinged with a touch of negativity

SILVER the psychic colour, protective, justice

GOLD wisdom

As you look at the colours, let yourself get a sense of what they mean to you.

Symbolically *draw* your strength and weakness and notice what colours you use:

A mandala is a sacred symbol of wholeness. It is a circle. *Draw* a mandala and fill it with beautiful colours of your choice. Do it as an offering to the Source, and focus on beauty as you do so. This will automatically raise your vibrations.

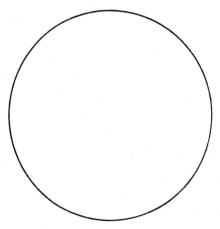

Understanding the chakras

Chakras are the spiritual energy centres of the body. Their purpose is to take in vibrations, feelings and energies, and purify and transform them.

The word chakra means 'wheel or circle' in Sanskrit and there are little tiny ones all over the surface of the body. However we are talking about the seven main chakras.

These are:

The base chakra at the base of the spine, which is red.

The sacral chakra in the abdomen, which is orange.

The solar plexus chakra in the solar plexus, which is yellow.

The heart chakra, in the centre of the chest, which is green.

The throat chakra, in the throat, which is blue.

The third eye chakra in the middle of the forehead, which is indigo.

The crown chakra, at the top of the head, which is violet.

In a spiritually undeveloped person they are like dull discs. Then, as we develop spiritually, they grow bigger and brighter and open like flowers on a stalk.

The stalk runs up our spine and each of the chakras is attached to the stalk by a little stem. When they are balanced and working perfectly, the chakras spin.

If a chakra is filled with negativity it closes and stops rotating, just like any wheel if blocked with dirt. And where we hold tension or fear, the relevant chakra stays closed. Old unhealed memories, hurts and angers clog up these energy centres and this stops the energy of the Universe flowing through us. Eventually we will manifest physical illness if we don't do something about it.

The lower three chakras are concerned with material, physical and sexual aspects of our lives and also with learning. We are out of balance if we are only interested in these things.

The upper chakras are to do with psychic and spiritual matters and of

course we are equally out of balance if we are only flowing in these centres.

Our aim on the Earth plane is to balance all our chakras. When they are clear, open and balanced, the Universal Energy flows through us. Then the kundalini energy, our life force, can rise up to our crown centre, which opens us up to enlightenment or illumination.

As we open more and more, we raise our vibrations and our light shines more brightly. Then we can be seen more clearly by those advanced beings in spirit who want to help us. They can only bring their vibrations down to a certain level and cannot help us until we raise ours to that level.

As each chakra is a colour of the rainbow, when each one is spinning in total harmony we become white light.

Testing the chakras

This is an exercise to do with the help of a friend to find out which of your chakras needs attention.

Where we have a weakness, the weak energy of that chakra will flow through to the arm muscle, so that we can test where we are weak by the following means. This test will also indicate where we are strong.

Stand in a relaxed way with your left hand on your crown chakra. Hold your right arm out parallel to the floor. Your friend tells you when she is about to push your arm down and you resist the pressure. If your chakra is weak your arm will drop under the push. If your chakra is strong your arm muscle will be strong enough to resist the pressure.

Do each chakra in the same way. Your friend must use the same amount of pressure for each one and you must resist with equal energy.

Record what you have discovered:

The lower chakras

The base or root chakra (red)

In a man this is at the base of the spine and in a woman it is between her ovaries. This is our survival chakra where we hold our primitive fears about money, food, unemployment, disasters, rape, etc. If we are worried about money, for example, we tense this chakra and our lower back suffers. Balancing this chakra calms our central nervous system and reduces tension in the spine, kidneys and adrenals.

When we balance this chakra we are grounded. If we are too yin we are ungrounded, impressionable or out of touch. We may get diarrhoea. When we are too yang we are too controlled, so we hang on, or work too hard. We block our creativity and have a tendency to constipation.

This is where our kundalini energy lies. This is our life force, our zest, our energy to do and accomplish. When this centre is open and spinning freely, our life flows with material success and creativity.

The sacral or spleen chakra (orange)

This is situated in our abdomen. Here we hold our attitudes to sin and guilt, sexual desire and sensual pleasures. So this is our emotional and sexual chakra. It is also very much connected to food.

Balancing this chakra helps all female problems, from menstruation to menopause to PMT. It regulates the fluids of the body, calms the bladder and eases arthritis and blood diseases.

Our lesson is to get the right balance between giving and receiving, sexually and emotionally. If we are too yin, sexually we tend towards frigidity or impotence. With food we might become anorexic. If we are too yang we could be over-sexual for our own nature or overweight.

When the energy in this chakra flows freely we are balanced sexually, original, creative. If we are psychic in this centre we will be clairsentient and pick up people's feelings, which means we could get emotionally drained or even pick up their physical pain. We need to learn to raise our energy to higher chakras.

The solar plexus chakra (yellow)

This is our personal power centre, where we hold our self-confidence and self-esteem. Fears of not being good enough, or not being liked, tense up this chakra because it is linked to the mind. Balancing this centre helps illnesses like cancer or tumours, which are based on internalised anger. The liver, spleen, gall bladder and stomach are all affected by this chakra.

When we are too yin we feel powerless and therefore angry. When we are too yang we become aggressive and greedy. When in balance we accept ourselves and everyone else. This is the central psychic point of the body. If this is out of balance we can feel sick and generally out of harmony.

Take a few moments to tune into these chakras in your body. If you could see them, what would they be like? *Draw* them as you imagine they look:

The upper chakras

The heart chakra (green)

This is our love centre, where we hold Christ consciousness in our bodies. Opening and balancing this centre allows us to heal heart problems and improve our circulation. It helps problems with the chest and shoulders.

The lesson here is love, social conscience and openness. If we are too yin here we are over-sensitive and if too yang we are insensitive. Either way we are closed down and focused on ourselves. When our heart is open we have true empathy and compassion and unconditional love.

The throat chakra (blue)

This is our centre of communication. Balancing this centre helps all throat problems, from colds and sore throats to laryngitis and thyroid problems.

When we swallow words and feelings, instead of vocalising them, this centre closes. We can even hold emotions down in our chest if we don't release them by speaking them out.

If we are too yin we find it hard to express ourselves openly and freely. If we are too yang we talk too much.

This is a very sensitive spiritual centre. The throat is the chakra of clairaudience where we tune into our guidance. So we hear our inner voice here and we have to discriminate between the true clear voice of truth and the voices of conditioning. Our lesson here is to discriminate between them so that we can find true understanding.

The third eye chakra (indigo)

The third eye is in the centre of the forehead between the brows. It is the chakra of high mental healing and clairvoyance. When it is out of balance we may get headaches or have difficulty concentrating.

When this centre is open and flowing we can see with our inner eye and focus our concentrated thought forms to heal others or to raise the vibrations of difficult situations. When we free this chakra we have enormous power and must pray for the wisdom to balance it.

The crown chakra (violet)

This is on the top of the head, where kings, queens and religious dignitaries wear their crowns to symbolise their link to the Highest. It is often depicted as a thousand-petalled lotus. This centre is where we are linked to the Universe and to our Source.

If we are out of balance here we feel generally unbalanced, for we are not aligned to our Higher Self. Our lesson here is absolute trust and submission to God.

When we work from this centre we work with pure intuition. This means we don't see auras, etc; we just know. It is the highest form of service to be in this state of knowingness.

Close your eyes and relax. Tune into each centre in turn, starting with the heart centre. Then *draw* what you would see if you could see your chakras:

Visualisation to strengthen the chakras

Find time and space to do this exercise. It is very important to balance you and get you into alignment with the Divine Power.

You may like to record this visualisation on to a tape or ask a friend to read it to you.

Sit in a chair with your spine straight or, if you prefer, sit cross-legged on the floor.

Breathe comfortably, imagining the outbreath stroking your spine until it feels very relaxed.

Imagine that your spine is a stalk. First let a grounding cord go down from your spine into the earth. It doesn't matter if you are upstairs, or even at the top of a block of flats, the cord simply goes through all matter into the earth. This grounds you and you may like to sense roots growing from it into the earth.

When you are rooted in the earth, sense that each chakra is a flower on the stalk. One at a time, check that each flower is straight and aligned on the stalk. Where they are out of alignment, picture them being gently pulled back straight. You may feel a physical difference in your body as you do this.

Breathe deeply into the base chakra. Imagine a bright, clear, red flower opening here. When it is fully open go inside it and clean it out. Old pictures, old memories or old feelings may come up. These have been clogging the chakra. Either pull them out and give them to the Universe to deal with or flush them down the grounding cord into the earth.

When the chakra is clear and clean, fill it with light and set it gently spinning.

Move up through the chakras, relaxing, opening, cleaning out each one, then filling it with light and rotating it. Remember, after the red chakra, comes the orange one in the abdomen, then the yellow one in the solar plexus,

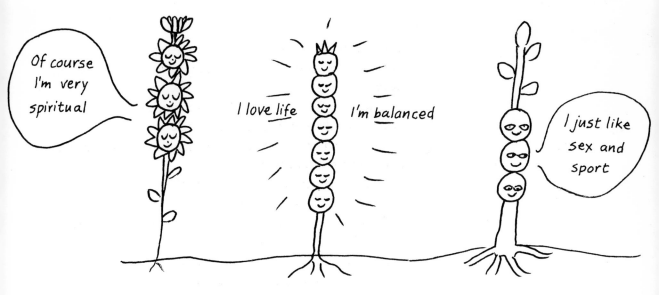

then the green one in the heart centre, the blue one in the throat, the indigo one at the third eye and the violet one like a crown at the top of your head.

When you have completed this imagine yourself radiating all the beautiful colours of the rainbow. As the colours of the rainbow spin and rotate, you become white light. You are perfect, shining, white light.

Breathe in this beautiful white light and know that when you are in this state you are connected to your Higher Self. Take time to experience this feeling and be aware of any thoughts or impressions that come to you.

1 *Note* your impressions:

_____

2 Repeat the exercise on page 166 and notice how much stronger each chakra is after the visualisation.

_____

_____

Journey up the chakras

Here is an inspirational journey up the chakras. As you go on this inner journey, your consciousness will be raised and your chakras will become brighter and clearer. So close your eyes and relax. Breathe gently until you are in a quiet meditative state.

You are in a green meadow. Look carefully around and notice what the meadow is like. This is the starting point for your journey up the spiritual mountain.

You are walking now towards the lowest slopes of the mountain, feeling vibrant with hope and expectation. Feel the earth under your feet. Be aware of the smell of red roses. You are surrounded by bright red flowers. Sit on a log or a bench amongst them and breathe in strength, courage, energy.

Move on higher, feeling happy and joyous, until you see all kinds of orange flowers around you. Here you are pausing to create a flower bed in the soil and planting beautiful new seeds. Water them lovingly, bless them and move on.

You are reaching the yellow level and you can see great drifts of golden daffodils. There is a blazing fire and you can sit by it. Place your fears on pieces of paper and throw each one into the flames and watch them dissolve. Breathe in power, confidence and self-worth until it feels as if the fire is within you.

With quiet assurance you are climbing up to a beautiful green plateau. The grass is soft and inviting. Touch it with your toes and feel it. Be aware of the breeze, gently blowing through your hair. You can hear the leaves rustling in the trees. You can sense the cosmic Christ enter the plateau, looking with love towards you. Your heart feels expanded and open and full of peace. You are at one with everyone.

After resting, move up to the beautiful turquoise blue lake you can now see. The water is crystal clear. Undress and float in the water. Time seems suspended as you are cleansed and purified. Focus on truth and faith until you get out of the water and dress again.

Higher still, there are blue flowers and a sense of deep peace. A waterfall cascades and tinkles over the rocks. Sit here and wait for a wise guide to appear. When he does, listen to what you are told. Ask your guide's name and know that when you use the vibration of his name, you are closer to your spiritual guidance.

Move to the top of the mountain. Stand on the pinnacle and open your arms. Be aware of the light from the Infinite Mind flowing into your consciousness. Experience oneness.

Gradually move down through the levels. Drink from the waterfall on the way down. How have your seeds grown? Tend and water them again.

Return to the meadow and relax. Open your eyes when you are ready.

Draw your journey through the chakras:

Index

About the author

Diana Cooper runs transformational workshops and courses in personal development and healing.
For details, please write to her at:

12 Frobisher Gardens
Guildford
Surrey GU1 2NT

Piatkus Books

If you have enjoyed reading this book, you may be interested in other titles published by Piatkus. These include:

As I See It: A psychic's guide to developing your healing and sensing abilities   Betty F. Balcombe

Awakening to Change: A guide to self-empowerment in the new millennium   Soozi Holbeche

Care Of The Soul: How to add depth and meaning to your everyday life   Thomas Moore

Child of Eternity, A: An extraordinary girl's message from the world beyond   Adriana Rocha and Kristi Jorde

Full Catastrophe Living: How to cope with stress, pain and illness using mindfulness meditation   Jon Kabat-Zinn

Handbook For The Soul: A collection of writings from over 30 celebrated spiritual writers   Richard Clarkson and Benjamin Shields (eds.)

Journey of Self-Discovery: How to work with the energies of chakras and archetypes   Ambika Wauters

Karma and Reincarnation: The key to spiritual evolution and enlightenment   Dr Hiroshi Motoyama

Light Up Your Life: And discover your true purpose and potential   Diana Cooper

Meditation For Every Day: Includes over 100 inspiring meditations for busy people   Bill Anderton

Message of Love, A: A channelled guide to our future   Ruth White

Messenger, The: The journey of a spiritual teacher   Geoff Boltwood

Mindfulness Meditation for Everyday Life   Jon Kabat-Zinn

Nostradamus – The Final Reckoning: A year-by-year guide to our future   Peter Lemesurier

River of Life, The: A guide to your spiritual journey   Ruth White

Stepping Into The Magic: A new approach to everyday life   Gill Edwards

Teach Yourself To Meditate: Over 20 simple exercises for peace, health and clarity of mind   Eric Harrison

Three Minute Meditator, The: 30 simple ways to relax and unwind   David Harp with Nina Feldman

Time for Healing, A: The journey to wholeness   Eddie and Debbie Shapiro

Time For Transformation, A: How to awaken to your soul's purpose and claim your power   Diana Cooper

Toward A Meaningful Life: The wisdom of the Rebbe Menachem Mendel Schneersohn   Simon Jacobson (ed.)

Transform Your Life: A step-by-step programme for change   Diana Cooper

Working With Guides And Angels   Ruth White

Working with Your Chakras   Ruth White

For a free brochure with further information on our full range of titles, please write to:

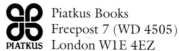

Piatkus Books
Freepost 7 (WD 4505)
London W1E 4EZ